Tilly

A Story of Hope
and Resilience

MONIQUE GRAY SMITH

sononis
PRESS
WINLAW, BRITISH COLUMBIA

Copyright © 2013 by Monique Gray Smith

LIBRARY AND ARCHIVES CANADA CATALOGUING IN PUBLICATION

Gray Smith, Monique, 1968–, author

    Tilly : a story of hope and resilience / Monique Gray Smith.

Originally published under title: Hope, faith & empathy.

ISBN 978-1-55039-209-8 (pbk.)

    I. Title. II. Title: Hope, faith & empathy.

PS8613.R3894T55 2013   C813'.6   C2013-901976-6

First Edition, 2012 by Little Drum Consulting
Second Edition, 2013

Sono Nis Press most gratefully acknowledges support for our publishing program provided by the Government of Canada through the Canada Book Fund and the Canada Council for the Arts, and by the Province of British Columbia through the British Columbia Arts Council and the Book Publishing Tax Credit, Ministry of Provincial Revenue.

Edited by Barbara Pulling
Copy edited by Dawn Loewen
Proofread by Audrey McClellan
Cover and interior design by Frances Hunter
Dragonfly artwork by Simone Diamond
    Courtesy of Native Northwest, Vancouver, Canada.

Published by
Sono Nis Press
Box 160
Winlaw, BC V0G 2J0
1-800-370-5228
books@sononis.com
www.sononis.com

Distributed in the U.S. by
Orca Book Publishers
Box 468
Custer, WA 98240-0468
1-800-210-5277

The Canada Council | Le Conseil des Arts
for the Arts | du Canada

Printed and bound in Canada by Houghton Boston Printing.
Printed on acid-free paper that is forest friendly (100% post-consumer recycled paper) and has been processed chlorine free.

For my children, Sadie and Jaxson:

May you always know you are the most precious gifts I have ever been blessed with. Walk gently wherever you may go, take good care of each other and always remember: be respectful and have fun! I love you.—Momma

CONTENTS

PREFACE

This book is loosely based on my own life story. The people you'll meet in these pages are a combination of individuals who showed up at pivotal times in my life to guide and teach me and characters who came to me as I wrote. These characters, I believe, are gifts from the Ancestors.

In telling Tilly's story, I illustrate different aspects of our collective Indigenous history in Canada. I am hopeful my book will also reveal how that history ripples into the current circumstances facing our people. The mere fact that Indigenous peoples exist in Canada is a miracle. That we are thriving in the multitude of ways we are is pure inspiration. I offer much gratitude to you, the reader, for sharing your time by reading this book. I hope you will find whatever you may be seeking as you join Tilly on her journey. And I hope you will encounter yourself: your own strength and resiliency. Perhaps, even just a little, Tilly's story will bring you closer to achieving your own dreams, ambitions and heart's desires.

Why did I choose the words *hope* and *resilience* for the subtitle of the book? For too many generations, Aboriginal people in Canada have experienced immense challenges. As a result, there has been significant trauma in the lives of our children. It is my hope that children of this generation and future generations will not have a childhood they have to recover from. I also have faith in the resiliency of the human spirit, faith that we can work together as Aboriginal and non-Aboriginal people to create a future that recognizes the gifts of all members of society.

Over the course of the story, I have used various terms to refer to the First Peoples of Canada: Indian, Native, Aboriginal, First Nations, Indigenous. The terminology has changed over time and I have chosen the terms most suitable to various situations and the various stages of Tilly's life. The glossary at the back of the book (p.197) gives more details about these and other terms.

At the back of the book you will also find a diagram, the Umbrella of First Nations Resiliency (p.205). There is a long, beautiful story about how this Umbrella came about, but in essence it is a visual that provides insight into some of the key historical events and legislative decisions that have impacted and continue to impact the First Peoples of Canada. The top part of the Umbrella contains the historical events and dates; the raindrops (or teardrops as many have said to me) are the impacts history continues to have; and the four words at the handle are the four keys to our resiliency. I acknowledge that each reader will have dates to add to the Umbrella, and this is one of the exciting aspects of this diagram as it creates reflection, dialogue and an exchange of knowledge.

And finally, on page 206, I have included a list of questions for book clubs or high school groups to use as a means of helping stimulate discussion.

WITH GRATITUDE

The book you hold in your hands is a dream come true. As with all dreams that become reality, it required hard work, support and encouragement from many individuals. I am beyond grateful for all who have encouraged my writing and the creation of *Tilly: A Story of Hope and Resilience*. This acknowledgements section has been the hardest part of the book to write, since words on paper don't seem to do justice to the gratitude I have in my heart.

I am incredibly grateful to my family; my happiest times in life are when we are all together. I am immensely appreciative of your support, love, encouragement and laughter. To my partner, Rhonda, thank you for always being my safe place to land. Thank you for putting up with my sleepless nights when I get up to write and for encouraging me to go after my dreams. Thank you to my children: Sadie, for sharing your wisdom, compassion and joyfulness; and Jaxson, for sharing your zest for life, humour and kindness. I adore you both.

To my mom, thank you for instilling in me important values of respect, honesty and hard work. I so admire you and appreciate all you have done for me over the years. You are quite extraordinary. To my sister, Teresa, thank you, quite simply, for being my sister, for all the beauty you bring to our family and the world, for always checking in on me, and for bringing Brianna into our lives. To my dad, thank you for sharing your business savvy and your love for sports and the outdoors.

To my dear friend Kelly Terbasket, *mi socia*, thank you for over twenty years of friendship and for bringing such light, adventure and humour to my life. I look forward to sharing stories on warm, sunny beaches for many years to come.

Thank you to the friends who read my initial writing and offered feedback, insights and guidance: Dena Carroll, Michelle Currie, Alison Gerlach, Mary Gordon, Diane Longboat, Shannon Lundquist, Onowa McIvor, Julie Paul, Christina Rumsey and Kelly Terbasket.

To Della Preston, thank you for your support of our family, especially for the integral role you have played in helping raise up our children.

I am incredibly grateful to Diane Morriss and Sono Nis Press for their belief in this book and in me as a writer. Diane, I am immensely appreciative of the collaborative approach you took through each stage of the book's development, and I eagerly anticipate what is next in our work together. Thank you to Nikki Tate for your support, guidance and leadership. Thank you to Frances Hunter for your creativity and craftsmanship in the cover and book design.

One of the greatest blessings in the creation of this book has been working with editor extraordinaire Barbara Pulling. I have grown immensely as a writer and a human being from working with you, and for that I am eternally grateful. I am also incredibly appreciative of Dawn Loewen. Your exquisite skills in copy editing and cultural understanding were beyond what I could have ever hoped for! I would also like to acknowledge and thank Simone Diamond, the artist whose beautiful dragonflies we used from her art card called, *Transforming Spirits*.

For more than twenty years, I have had the privilege of working in First Nations, urban Aboriginal and Métis communities across Canada, and it is the individuals and families I meet in this work who inspire and motivate me. I am in awe of the resilience of our people, and that awe was my inspiration for this book.

To those who have gone before me, my Ancestors, thank you for helping me so profoundly and for watching over me.

With respect,
Monique

CHAPTER 1

A Scary Encounter

I HUNG ON TO MY MOM'S PINKY as I skipped along the sidewalk, my curly, dark brown pigtails bouncing rhythmically. It was 1974 and a typical summer day in Kelowna. The sun shone brightly, the smell of ripe fruit hung in the air and the streets were bustling with tourists loading up on supplies before they headed to their fancy cabins on Okanagan Lake. We had left my tagalong sister, Marie, at home, and I was thrilled to have Mom all to myself. For that hour, she was mine. I knew if I didn't ask to go to the toy section at Kmart, listened to her and stayed out of her way while she shopped, a stop at Monty's ice cream shop would be in the cards for me. Monty had the best homemade ice cream in Kelowna, and he double-dipped my chocolate cone for me every time. "Just to match your big brown eyes, there, little beauty," he would say as he handed me the delicious cone.

I wasn't really paying attention to where Mom and I were going. I was more interested in watching my pigtails take turns flying in front of my eyes. All of a sudden, Mom's pinky slipped out of my hand, and I ran into something solid. I was thrown off my feet, landing with such force on the sidewalk that the wind was knocked out of me. Worn-out cowboy boots were what I saw as I tried to catch my breath. When I looked up, the sun stung my eyes, and all I could make out was the hugest belly I had ever seen.

"Jesus Christ, kid, you ran right into me." In one swift move, the man yanked me up by the elbow and shoved me towards my mom. "Goddamn squaw. Get control of your kid or go back to the reserve. Back where you belong. And stay there!"

He spat these words at my mom, then pushed past her and continued on his way. Mom gasped, then went silent as she stared down at the sidewalk. I looked over my shoulder, wisps of hair falling in my eyes. I was happy to see him walking away.

I didn't really know what had just gone on, but that man, he scared me. I felt like I was going to throw up, and I needed to pee, badly. As we started walking again, I reached for Mom's baby finger, but now it was as cold as an icicle, and her hand shook so hard I had trouble hanging on to it. I was afraid to look at her. Out of the corner of my eye, I saw her quickly wiping away tears. She didn't seem quite as tall as she'd been before. I waited until her pinky felt warm before I said anything.

"Momma, why was he so mean?" I asked. "Momma, what does *squaw* mean?"

Mom's chin trembled, and a tear slid down her face. I let go of her finger and held on to her whole hand. I needed to feel more of her. "I'm sorry I made you cry, Momma."

Mom squeezed my hand. "Let's just go home, Tilly. Momma's not feeling so good."

I knew that meant no trip to Monty's and no ice cream cone for me today. Now I was even madder at that man.

Mom must have called Auntie Pauline, my dad's oldest sister, as soon as we got home because it wasn't long until my auntie came over to visit. She and her family lived in Kamloops, about two hours away, but they had come to Kelowna for a holiday and were staying with my auntie's friend from work. When Auntie Pauline arrived that day, she was alone. I wondered where my cousins were. She and Mom sat out on the deck talking, and I tried to hear what was going on, but they kept sending me out to play with Marie.

Auntie was still there when it was time for bed, so I asked her to tuck me in. After reading to me for a bit, she pulled the covers up and tucked them under my chin, kissed me on my nose and forehead and turned out the light. Just as she was about to close my door, I squeaked out a question: "Auntie, what does *squaw* mean?"

She came and sat on the side of my bed. "Oh, my girl. I'm so sorry that happened to you and your mom today."

"But what does it mean, Auntie? And why was that man so mean to us?"

Auntie Pauline crawled into bed with me. I nuzzled into her as she ran her fingers through my hair. I was cozy, almost asleep. Then, in a whisper, she began, "Tilly, your momma is a very special woman. You need to remember that. She loves you and your sister more than anything in the world.

Sometimes big people are hard to understand. Your momma, she's had some really hard times in her life."

"Is that why sometimes she gets quiet for lots of days and we get to eat Kentucky Fried Chicken?"

"Well, my girl, that's one of the reasons."

"But Auntie, why won't anyone tell me what *squaw* means?"

She was quiet for a bit. "It's a word used for Indian women. Not a very nice word."

"Why did that man say it to Momma?"

"You see, Tilly, your momma's an Indian woman. She knows she's from the Cree Nation, but she doesn't know who her family is because she was taken away from them when she was a baby."

"Taken away from her mom and dad?" I didn't understand. "Why, Auntie?"

"Oh, my girl, you always have so many questions." She kissed the top of my head, smoothed my bangs on my forehead. "Things were different back then, Tilly. Her mom and dad were really young, and they couldn't take care of her. So she was put in a place for babies who don't have families. She lived there until she was almost as old as you are now. Then your grandma and grandpa came and took your mom home to live with them as part of *their* family. They adopted her. Your grandma and grandpa, oh, how they loved your momma. But they didn't understand how important it was for her to know her culture or her language. And because of the adoption rules back then, they didn't know what community your mom was from or who her family was. But your momma has always known she is Cree."

"But what does it mean to be Cree?" I asked.

"That's not a question I can answer. I'm not Cree. But as you know, Grandma Tilly, your daddy and I are part Lakota. I don't know very much about that part of me either. Even though Grandma Tilly tried to teach us about being Lakota and told us to feel proud, I never really did. Especially once I got to school, and all the kids made fun of us and of her. I felt ashamed." Auntie Pauline let out a deep breath, then continued. "I'm hoping that one day you can ask your mom about being Cree and that she might want to find out more about her Cree ways. If it's okay with her, I'll help you find out more whenever you want to. And maybe I can learn a little bit more about being Lakota and share that with you."

I was trying to figure all this out. "Does it mean that I'm Cree, too?" I asked, hopeful. I wanted to be as much like my mom as possible.

"Yes, my girl, it does. And I want you to be proud of that. You come from very strong people." Auntie Pauline turned my face so I could look up at her. "You are a special little girl, and there are many, many people who love you." She tucked the covers around me as she slid out of my bed. "It's been a big day for you, my girl. You need to have a good sleep. I'm gonna go home in a bit, but I'll come visit tomorrow."

As she was about to close the door, she blew me a final kiss. "Sweet dreams, and don't let the bedbugs bite. If they do, hit them with your shoe." I giggled as I imagined squishing the little bugs with my big shoe.

I woke the next morning to our cat, Midnight, curled around my head and the sound of gentle snoring in my ear.

Someone was lying beside me. I rolled over, and there was Momma. I loved it when she slept with me. It didn't happen often. As the sun peeked through the opening in my curtains, I looked at her face. Her nose was long and straight, her cheeks were big and round, and her skin was the same colour as chocolate milk, and so soft. She was the most beautiful woman in the world.

Sometimes I heard my mom crying in her bedroom or in the bathtub. But I hardly ever saw her cry, and yesterday had scared me. As I carefully crawled out from under the covers, Midnight stretched and repositioned herself at the top of Momma's head. I scooched my way to the edge of the bed and put on my slippers.

When I opened my bedroom door, the smell of bacon and pancakes surprised me. In the kitchen, my dad was making breakfast. I went over and wrapped my arms around his waist. "Why are you making breakfast, Daddy? It's not Sunday."

He rested his hand on my shoulder. "Your momma didn't sleep very good last night, Tilly."

We were both quiet for a moment. I leaned my head against his side. "Was it because of that mean man?"

"Don't you go worrying your little self about it. I think your momma will spend the day in bed, so I want you to make sure you and your sister keep the noise down for her. You can play outside for the day."

Later that morning, Marie and I were in the backyard on our swing set when Auntie Pauline came over with our cousins, Eddie, Millie and Mark.

"Hey, Tilly, where's your mom?" Auntie Pauline asked as she peeked her head into the backyard.

"She's in her room, I think."

"I'm gonna go in and check on her, but why don't you girls go and get your swimsuits on and you can come down to the lake with us."

"Woo hoo!" Marie and I both jumped off the swings and ran past Auntie Pauline into the house. I could hardly wait to jump into the lake and practise my underwater handstands.

CHAPTER 2

Grandma Tilly

WE NEVER KNEW EXACTLY WHEN Grandma Tilly would arrive, but the moment her car pulled up, it was as if she cast a spell of excitement over our family. Grandma Tilly drove all by herself from her farm near Regina to visit us. "When the spirit moves me," she'd say, "I get in my car, fill up the tank and start drivin'." It had to be good weather, though. Grandma never came to see us in the winter. "No way I'm drivin' through the mountains when there's snow," she told us. Sometimes I felt like I lived for her visits, phone calls and letters.

Grandma Tilly wasn't quite five feet tall. She had big chocolate-brown eyes, and her face was covered with wrinkles that seemed to float into their rightful place whenever she smiled or laughed—which was often. Her hair was silver, always worn in a braid. She was constantly tucking wisps of it behind her ears, wisps that refused to be contained, much like Grandma herself. She was feisty, funny and generous. It was her way to share what she had and to ensure the Elders and children around her always had what they needed. She wasn't simply full of love, kindness and joy—she *was* love, kindness and joy.

Grandma Tilly was also ahead of her time. She was well read and a university graduate—which for a woman of her generation, especially an Indian woman, was remarkable. Grandma loved telling the story of how her family supported her and how she knew many went without so that she could get her bachelor's degree in science.

After she'd given birth to my dad, her fourth of thirteen children, she gave up on her dream of becoming a medical doctor. She focused instead on taking care of her family and running the farm. But she continued to practise the healing ceremonies and use the traditional medicines she'd learned about from her grandfather. Many people saw her as a healer.

During one summer visit, while Grandma Tilly was having her evening pipe, she told me, "You know, Tilly, I was about ten when I first started learnin' about books."

"Really?" I asked. "Didn't you have to go to school?"

"Oh, I was learnin' every single day, but I never went to no school in a building till I was sixteen. My school was the land, the rivers, the stars, our ceremonies, and my grandma and grandpa. They taught me so much on our farm back there in Saskabush that I never woulda learned in school. They taught me how to hunt and fish, how to cook whatever we caught, when to harvest medicines and what to use 'em for, and how to know which plants and berries you could eat. I hear lots of our people today talk about learning how to live off the land. But back then it wasn't something we talked about; we just did it in order to survive. My grandma and grandpa, they didn't speak any English, so I only spoke Lakota with them. My grandpa, well, he was what I guess today you'd call a medicine man. I was his helper."

With us, Grandma Tilly spoke with an accent—some might call it slang. But when she was out in public, she spoke proper English and her accent disappeared. The first time I noticed this, we were at the mall in Kelowna. My eighth birthday was coming up, and she had taken me to Sears to pick out a new fishing rod.

I was puzzled when I heard Grandma Tilly talking to the salesperson. It was her voice, but she sounded so different.

After we left the store, she took my hand. "My girl, I saw how you looked at me in there, like you was confused by how I talked to the lady. I know I sounded a bit different than usual, but I'm still the same person." She directed us to a bench, and once we were settled she looked me in the eyes.

"You see, when I was growin' up, there was lots of meanness to our people, an' my daddy didn't want me to experience any o' that. So he taught me how to speak proper English. It was very important to him that I was never judged because o' my accent from speakin' Indian. An' to tell you the truth, Tilly, I love watchin' people's reaction when I talk to 'em, most times with better English than they speak. They're usually shocked to see an old Indian woman speakin' to 'em like I do." She chuckled as she gave my hand a squeeze. "Way back in university, I learned how important it was to challenge people's assumptions 'bout us as Indian people." Her voice got softer, full of sadness. "Unfortunately, most o' my kids got influenced from school an' society an' aren't real proud of bein' Indian. That's why I'm tryin' to help you and your sister be proud of who you are. I'm trying to get your dad to be proud, too, but that's up to him. Times are changin' for us as Indian people, Tilly. Today more an' more of our people, well, they are proud to be Indian, and that is a good thing—a real good thing."

I left the mall that day loving my Grandma Tilly more than ever.

CHAPTER 3

Kamloops

A COUPLE OF WEEKS AFTER one of Grandma Tilly's visits, my dad told us at dinner he had a surprise announcement to make. Marie and I looked at each other with wide eyes, wondering with excitement what it could be. "We're moving to Kamloops," he said with his chest pushed out and his head held higher than usual.

Mom's fork fell onto her plate loudly, startling us. Her face was red, and her bottom lip was trembling.

"What the hell, George. Another move?" Mom said. Her voice got louder. "What are you going to do there for work?"

"I've been offered a real good sales job at the Ford dealership," Dad said in his usual calm way. "I start in three weeks."

Marie and I looked at each other again. Our excitement was gone, replaced now by fear. We hated it when Mom used bad words or was mad at Daddy.

"Nice of you to consult your family about your decision, George." Mom stood up abruptly, her chair toppling over behind her. She stormed off to their room, slamming the door behind her.

For the next few days, Mom tucked herself away in their room and refused to talk to Dad. Marie and I took care of her, bringing her food and tea. She'd come out only when Dad left the house, and she refused to help with any of our preparations for moving.

Even though he had to sleep on our uncomfortable couch, Dad didn't appear too worried about all this. "Your momma will come around. She'll see it's a good idea for us to move. She just needs a bit of time." He wasn't a great cook, so we ate a lot of frozen pizzas and hamburger soup.

Dad showed Marie and me how to pack boxes, and the three of us did the work of getting ready for the move. It was hot in the house, and packing was no fun. I just wanted to be outside, running through the sprinkler or riding my bike.

Moving always created angst in me. I should have gotten used to it, because we'd moved ten times since I was born, but I never did. I wasn't very good at making friends, and the loneliness of a new school only made me feel worse that I hadn't yet found a place where I felt like I belonged.

I had made a few friends in Kelowna, but because it was summer vacation I hadn't seen much of them. Now we were moving and I'd never see them again. There was no chance to even say goodbye.

The only good thing about our move to Kamloops was that Auntie Pauline, Uncle Mike and our cousins lived there. Grandma Tilly announced she was coming again to help us unpack and get set up in our new house.

Whenever Grandma was visiting, I'd wake full of anticipation. I knew a day of adventure and learning awaited me. She taught me how to hook a worm on my fishing rod, how to snare a rabbit, how to hold a baseball bat, how to load a pipe with tobacco so that it would be easy to smoke but not burn too fast, and how to stitch the hem on my pants. She taught me how to make tobacco offerings of gratitude and prayers, how to pick medicines and how to spot which plants in the forest were edible and which ones were poisonous.

Grandma Tilly and Marie had their own special relationship. The longest days for me when she was visiting were the days she spent alone with Marie, teaching my sister how to sew and bead, can fruit, make preserves, and create ointments from the medicines.

Even though Grandma explained why she taught us different things and spent time alone with each of us—because she saw our unique gifts, interests and talents, and she wanted to build on them—I was still jealous of her time with Marie, or with anyone else for that matter.

On special occasions, she'd take both of us out with her. We had been in Kamloops for only a few weeks when one afternoon she told Mom, "I'm gonna take the girls out on the land today. We'll be back in time for dinner."

We drove out to the reserve to visit Grandma Tilly's friend Dave. They'd met a few years earlier at an Elders' Gathering and had stayed in touch. He came out on the porch to greet us. "I've been waiting for the three of you," he said. "Come on in. I just finished makin' fry bread." Grandma had brought gifts for Dave: her tobacco, braids of sweetgrass and some of Mom's canned peaches and moose meat.

His fry bread was heavenly—each piece about an inch thick, the size of a hockey puck and fried to golden-brown perfection.

After we'd devoured it, Dave took us hiking up behind his house. He showed us the traditional medicines of his people, the Secwepemc. He was impressed that Marie and I had tobacco with us and knew how to make an offering before we picked any sage or other medicines.

During her visits, Grandma Tilly taught me about being generous, telling the truth and always treating other people with dignity and respect. Every night after dinner, she and I would sit outside, and she would pull out her pipe bag and load her pipe for her evening smoke. "C'mere, li'l Tilly, gather under my wing and let's talk about the day." With me tucked up close to her, we'd review our escapades. She'd ask me, "What'd you learn today? What was the best part?"

I missed her so much once she'd gone home, but Grandma Tilly made a point of staying in touch by phone. She was on a party line in her farm community, and it was common to be on a phone call with her and have someone cut in.

"Who's on the line?" the person would ask.

"It's Tilly. I'm on with li'l Tilly, an' we gonna be a while."

Once, when I called her to talk about some things I was upset about at school, she told me, "What you gotta remember, Tilly, is everyone's born with love in their hearts. Sometimes life takes that away, but we all born with it. So whenever you enter a room, in your imagination, fill it with love. And make enough room for everyone else to fill that room with love, too. That, my girl, is when good things happen."

I always felt better after my talks with Grandma Tilly. Her teachings, words and sayings were like medicine to me. I carried them in my heart to help me feel strong, and they reminded me of the powerful woman I was named after.

CHAPTER 4

Family Caravans

SOMETIMES MOMMA, DADDY, MARIE AND I would pile in our car and make the long trip to see Grandma Tilly. Along the way, we'd stop and pick up some of my uncles, aunts and cousins. We'd drive to Grandma Tilly's farm in a caravan of vehicles.

I loved travelling in a group like this. When we stopped, we kids could change cars, and that broke up the trip. Each family had their own fun ways to pass the time. Auntie Pauline and Uncle Mike loved to sing, especially country and western songs. My dad told stories: scary stories, funny stories, all kinds of stories. My Uncle Bob, who lived in Edmonton by himself and only made the trip with us a couple times, had a CB radio in his truck, and he'd allow us to play with it and talk with other truckers. We usually drove straight through to Grandma's farm near Regina, a whole twenty-four hours away, stopping only to pick up family, pee and get gas. My mom would pack enough food for the trip, but every so often when we'd stop to get gas, Dad would buy us a snack.

Grandma Tilly grew her own tobacco, starting each winter with sixteen seeds. She grew eight plants for her personal use, four to share with Elders and four for use in ceremonies and as offerings. She'd start the plants out in the house, then transfer them to her garden at the full moon in May. They were the most beautiful plants in the garden when they flowered.

Thanksgiving weekend was always tobacco harvesting time. Grandma Tilly would interrupt her harvesting to join the family for dinner, bringing in fresh tobacco to place on the plate that held the food offering. Other than that, she worked all weekend. Even though she only had sixteen plants, every step of harvesting those plants was precise and meticulous and always accompanied by prayer songs.

My cousins and I would sit in the barn for hours watching her tenderly harvest her tobacco plants, singing traditional songs as she worked.

"Can we help, Grandma?"

"The best way you can help me right now is to fill this barn with all the love in your hearts, so the medicine of your love goes into the tobacco." She'd come over and kiss our foreheads, pausing to give each of us our own special moment.

The year I was nine and Marie was six, our family got caught in a really bad snowstorm on our way to Grandma Tilly's for Christmas. There were just the four of us that time. My dad was leaning forward over the steering wheel, his hands gripping it tightly. His cigarette was a red glow. My mom had one hand on his shoulder. With the other she clung to the car door just below the window.

I was scared. It was starting to get dark, and every so often the wind would blow our car sideways. When I sat straight up and looked out the windshield, I could hardly see the road for the blowing snow.

"Medicine Hat is just a few more miles," Mom said in a barely audible voice. "Maybe we can get a motel room for the night."

Marie and I looked at each other. We had never stayed in a motel before, and for a moment our fear turned to excitement.

It seemed like a long time before we eased off the highway. "Everyone keep your eyes peeled for a motel with a sign that says Vacancy," Dad said. The snow didn't seem to be blowing as hard, and it was a bit easier to see.

"There, Daddy, over there." I reached forward from the back seat and pointed to the Lucky Seven Motel.

Dad pulled into the parking lot and turned to my mom.

"What do you think, hon?"

She raised her eyebrows. "Not sure we have much choice."

Dad opened the car door, and when he stepped out it sounded like Styrofoam was being squished beneath his feet. He disappeared into the stormy night. He came back covered in snow and waving a key.

"Well, girls, what do you say? Should we go check out our sleeping quarters for the night?"

"Yippee!" Marie and I squealed with pleasure.

The room smelled of cigarette smoke. It had two beds, a TV, a small table with two chairs, and a bathroom with a tiny tub. The carpet was torn in places, and the bedcovers had small black holes in them.

"You girls take those covers off and put our sleeping bags on the beds," my mom instructed.

"The woman at the front desk told me there's a Chinese restaurant with a buffet just around the corner," Dad said. "You know what else she told me?"

Marie and I shook our heads.

"She told me there's an old movie theatre beside the restaurant. Tonight it's showing *The Apple Dumpling Gang*."

Marie and I squealed again. The movie was a couple years old by then, but it didn't matter to us; we'd never seen it. We'd never been to a movie theatre at all.

We bundled up again and headed out into the night. My sister and I could hardly wait to get through dinner. A thrill went through me as we walked into the theatre. The smell of popcorn wafted around us, and the walls were covered with posters of old movies. I could barely contain my excitement when Dad said we could get popcorn and a Coke. Marie and I followed our parents into the dark theatre, carefully carrying our treats. I had a hard time figuring out how the seat worked, and Mom had to show me how to pull it down.

The theatre got even darker. The curtains opened, and on the huge screen the movie began. I loved every bit of it.

Back at the motel, just before I dropped off to sleep, I opened one eye and looked at Marie. She was sleeping with a smile on her face. I smiled, too. This had been the best night ever, and I couldn't wait to tell Grandma Tilly all about it.

CHAPTER 5

Making Ends Meet

I ALWAYS KNEW WHEN THERE WASN'T much money in our
house, because we'd eat a lot more moose meat goulash and
hamburger soup. Fried bologna and macaroni with canned
tomatoes were by far my favourite foods, next to chocolate
cake, of course. Sometimes Auntie Pauline would bring over
her homemade bread or cinnamon buns.

A hush fell over my parents during these lean times. They
rarely laughed, entertained friends or played cards. It seemed
as if we had to hit some kind of bottom before we started to
make a change. But once we did, my parents were ingenious
at finding ways to make ends meet. My mom sold her canning
and ceramics, and my dad always had money-making schemes
up his sleeve. The one I loved most was selling firewood.

On weekends we'd head out to the bush, all four of us
crammed in the cab of our beat-up Ford pickup with country
music blaring out of the speakers. My dad knew all the good
places to get wood, usually along old logging roads with a
steep drop on one side. He'd pull the truck over, get out

and wander up and down the road, looking at all the trees. We'd wait eagerly in the truck until he pointed up and yelled, "There it is. There's the one for today." Then we'd all clamber out to get a better look. The smell of the forest would envelop me. It always brought happy memories of my time out in the bush with Grandma Tilly.

"Okay, go get yourselves ready," Dad would say. "Tilly, bring me my gloves and saw." I'd run off to the back of the truck, lower the tailgate, climb in and push the chainsaw to the edge. Then I'd climb back out, tuck his gloves into my pants pockets and, summoning all my might, lift the saw and carry it over to where Dad was. If I was quick enough, I'd get there just as he was standing up from having placed tobacco at the base of the tree. It was the only time I ever saw him practise any of what Grandma Tilly had taught me. I was confused about why he felt he had to hide what he was doing.

Dad taught me how to see which way a tree was leaning and which other trees might be in the way as it fell. He trained me to use my finger to figure out which way the wind was blowing. Once we'd done that, he'd send me back up to the road. "Go stand with your mother and Marie while I cut this baby down." We'd wait excitedly for the noise of the saw to stop, because when it did we knew the best part was about to happen. Dad would yell up to us, "You all ready?"

"Yes!" we'd say in unison.

From where we were standing, we could see him put both his hands against the tree and begin to push. Sometimes he'd have to rock it a bit, but when he knew it was about to fall, he'd yell, "Tim-berrrr!" We'd watch in amazement as the tree broke through all the branches and greenery on its way down. Once it hit the ground, Marie and I would run down to join him.

"You girls start pulling off the branches up near the top, and I'll start sawing off the big ones down here," Dad instructed. Might not have been that safe, but it worked for us. Once all the branches were off, he'd saw the trunk into blocks about a foot long. Marie and I carried them up to the truck, and Mom piled them in the back. It always amazed me how she got all the blocks to fit together so they wouldn't move when we started driving.

When all the blocks and any pieces that could be used for kindling were loaded into the back of the truck, we'd climb in and sing along to the music as we drove to a nearby creek or lake. Dad knew where the good fishing spots were, too. After lunch, we'd pull out our rods and fish for a while. Mom and Dad were always in better moods on the days we caught fish.

Every so often, on our way back into town, Dad would treat us to a chocolate bar. My favourite was Cuban Lunch. Marie preferred Smarties, which she called brain candy. The treats kept us content and preoccupied all the way home.

CHAPTER 6

Gatekeepers to the Dream World

ONE JULY DAY WHEN I WAS ELEVEN, Grandma Tilly showed up just in time for dinner, after driving all the way from her farm. Secretly I had been expecting her. I'd written her a letter telling her that the sage was almost ready to pick and that I'd heard on the radio the fishing was unusually good this year.

She never mentioned my letter, just told my parents she'd come to take me fishing. "It's time to teach Tilly how to prepare for the winter. Best time for fishing all summer is this new moon." She winked at me across the dinner table. "So we're gonna pack up and spend a while up at the lake."

By noon the following day, we'd pitched our tent close to the lake. Dad had hauled up our twelve-foot aluminum boat for Grandma and me to use. He stayed to help us get our camp set up, though we didn't really need his help. I think he wanted to stay and fish with us, but Grandma Tilly shooed him off home.

That evening, Grandma Tilly taught me how to build a firepit and gather the wood we'd need. The next morning we established our routine for the week. We'd get up very early and fish until Grandma Tilly felt we had caught our share for the day. Then we'd head back to our camp, get the fire going and prepare the fish to be smoked. Grandma Tilly had her own special recipe for the brine, which included wild onions that she harvested every fall and preserved. The fish would sit in the brine for a couple of hours before we hung them over the fire. The smoked fish would be a treat throughout the winter. Now that Grandma Tilly was older and couldn't hunt anymore, she often traded her smoked fish for deer or moose meat.

It was my job to prepare the fish to go in the brine by scraping and gutting them. Then I'd hand them to Grandma, who would cut their heads off and put them into a container in the cooler. "Oh, your daddy and Auntie Pauline, they gonna be so happy with all the heads we got. I'm gonna make us up some of my famous fish head soup," Grandma Tilly said to me, smiling.

I gave her just a bit of a smile back. As I remembered the smell of that soup, I thought to myself, *I'm going to make sure I'm out of the house when that's cooking.*

Apparently there was a lot to be said for digging the meat out of a fish's head, and even more for extracting and sucking on an eyeball, but I was fine going through life without those particular pleasures.

We were sitting around the fire one night when Grandma Tilly announced, "Tomorrow, after we done fishin', we gonna go home. We'll stop and pick our sage and then we'll have enough fish and sage for the winter. It's not our way to be greedy. Just take what we need an' what we gonna share: nothin' more an' nothin' less." She pointed at me with her fire stoker. "This whole world gettin' so greedy, but not you. You only gonna take what you need an' what you gonna share, Tilly. You hear me?"

I nodded yes, knowing there was no other response. It wasn't very often Grandma Tilly spoke to me in such a forceful way, but when she did, I knew I'd better sit still and listen.

The next morning we got up early, as usual, and headed out onto the lake for our last day of fishing. The blue-grey mountains created stunning reflections on the water. The loons had begun to call, and frogs were croaking. Since it was summer vacation, I would normally be tucked into my bed for a few hours yet. But having this chance to spend time alone with Grandma Tilly made it worth getting up with the sun.

Soon Grandma had reeled in seven fish, but I was still waiting for my first one. And not just my first fish, my first bite! I started to whine. "Why are you catching all the…"

I didn't get to finish my question before she raised her hand, silencing me. I looked out over the lake. I should have known better than to complain to Grandma Tilly.

"Did you remember to do everythin' I been teachin' you?" she asked. She raised her eyebrows at me and pursed her lips.

I knew I'd better not answer without thinking seriously about her question, so I turned around to face the front of the boat. I watched as the bow broke through the water, leaving gentle ripples in its wake. We had been fishing every morning for a week, and I replayed in my mind the fishing preparations. Had I forgotten something this morning? As usual, I'd woken up, got dressed, rinsed my mouth, washed my face, helped pack up our gear, got in the boat. I couldn't figure it out. I stared at my rod, wishing with all my might it would bend towards the water.

I heard Grandma Tilly strike a wooden match on the side of the boat. Without turning around, I knew she was lighting her pipe. The breeze wafted the smell of her homegrown tobacco towards me.

"That's it, Grandma Tilly!" I turned quickly to face her, rocking the boat.

"*What's* it?" She puffed on her pipe. Whenever she exhaled she used her hand to send the smoke up over her head, as if she was smudging.

"I forgot to make my tobacco offering before we got in the boat." I was quiet for a moment, mad at myself for forgetting something so important. "That's why I'm not getting any bites or catching any fish."

"Yes, my girl. You forgot to make your offering. You figured that one out quick, Tilly. You must be my grand-daughter." She laughed, then continued in a more serious tone. "No offering, no fish. Simple law o' nature. We make the offering as a form of gratitude. Need to be grateful before we ask an animal to give up its life so we can eat."

I began reeling my line in, embarrassed at letting her down.

"Sorry, Grandma..."

But before I could finish, she shook her head.

41

"No need for apologizin', Tilly. This is a good lesson for you. I have a hunch you'll remember to make your tobacco offerings from now on. We got what we need now for the winter. Let's head back to camp and get these fish smoked so we can go pick our sage and then head home." She smacked her lips a couple times. "Got a cravin' for that fish head soup."

As we eased in to the dock, a dragonfly circled around my head. I didn't dare swat at it. "Oh, my, Tilly. You gonna have to pay real good attention to your dreams tonight. That dragonfly's come to remind you of that—we call 'em gatekeepers to the dream world."

Grandma Tilly's head turned as she followed the quick movements of the dragonfly. "You remember what I told you about dreams?"

"Sure I do," I said proudly. "The dreams I have when I first fall asleep are about my past. They'll help me learn from my past so I don't make the same mistakes. The ones in the middle of my sleep will help me solve whatever problems I have right now. And the dreams I have just before I wake up, those dreams are about the future. They'll help me get ready for what is to come."

"You been using those two ears real well, Tilly. I'm gonna be curious tomorrow to hear about the dreams you have tonight."

We sat there watching the dragonfly until it finally flew away. Grandma Tilly motioned towards the rope with her head. "Tie us up now, so we can start smokin' these fish."

CHAPTER 7

Losing My Anchor

THAT FALL I STARTED GRADE SEVEN. We lived close enough for me to walk, and one afternoon when I turned into our back alley, I saw my dad's truck in our driveway. "What's he doing home from work?" I wondered. As I got closer, I noticed that my Auntie Pauline's car was there, too. Not good.

Suddenly I found it hard to breathe, as if someone had hit me in the stomach with a baseball bat. My legs felt like Jell-O. I sat down at the entrance to our driveway. I couldn't go in. I just couldn't. I could smell her tobacco...Grandma Tilly.

"No, not Grandma Tilly," I prayed silently. "Anybody but Grandma Tilly, please! I'll listen to Mom and Dad, I'll do my homework, eat my vegetables, even be nice to my sister. But please, don't take Grandma Tilly away, not yet!"

It was one of my first attempted negotiations with the Creator. I don't know how long I stayed there; time seemed to stand still. Finally Mom came looking for me. She sat down beside me and gently moved me onto her lap. She tucked my head under her chin, encircled me with her arms and rocked me back and forth. My tears began to flow.

"Is it...is it...?"

"Yes, my girl." Mom's voice cracked. "Grandma Tilly passed away this morning." I could feel her chest moving beneath me, and I knew she was crying, too. Mom was not always emotionally available to me, but on this day, when I needed her most, she was there.

That night I lay in bed with tears streaming down my face. I wondered if anyone had called Grandma's friend Dave. Or maybe somehow he knew already, just like he'd always known to have his fry bread ready whenever we dropped in to visit.

Mom came into my room. "Tilly, I need your help to get your dad to bed and Auntie to the couch." Both Dad and Auntie Pauline had drowned their sorrows in a few too many drinks and passed out at the kitchen table.

In this life we all need someone, or the memory of someone, to help us through hard times. For me, that person was Grandma Tilly. After she died, there wasn't a day went by that I didn't think of her. In moments of reflection, I felt her with me. I knew she walked beside me, protecting me and guiding me. Some days I would feel her so close. When I closed my eyes, I'd imagine the two of us out on the porch again, Grandma Tilly puffing on her pipe, me tucked under her arm, safe and secure.

She'd been my anchor, and now she was gone.

CHAPTER 8

The Buzz

MY DAD AND HIS SIBLINGS DID WHAT they had seen their own father do: they drank to celebrate, they drank because it was a hot summer day, they drank because it was a cold winter's night, they drank when the Roughriders won or the Oilers lost. From the time my sister and I were young, we learned that when you were celebrating or when you were hurting—in fact, for pretty much any reason you created— you poured yourself a cold one.

Often my dad would let me have a swig of his beer, or Auntie Pauline would give me a taste of one of her "frou-frou" drinks: mai tais and pina coladas. Even though I found the taste of beer disgusting, I never let my dad know, for fear he wouldn't offer again. I felt like his special little girl when he let me have a swig. And I instantly liked the taste of my auntie's drinks. I learned that if I used a straw, I could slip it into her drink and take a long sip when she wasn't looking.

My real attachment to alcohol began in the spring of grade seven, when a couple of girls in my class, Abby and Jo, invited me to Abby's house for lunch. "Come on, Tilly," Abby said. "My parents are at work, but they left us something special."

As usual, I was finding it very hard to make friends. I was tired of eating my fried bologna sandwiches all alone and excited to be invited. Abby's place was close to our school, and I was surprised to see that her parents had left their alcohol sitting on the kitchen floor. My parents kept their liquor in the cupboard above the fridge, and my dad's beer was in the small fridge in the workshop. I watched as Abby mixed vodka, orange juice and 7UP. On my first sip, my tongue burned, and a warm sensation followed the liquid down to my stomach. The drink tasted so good that I gulped down the whole glass. "This is delicious. It's sort of like a Shirley Temple," I said to my new friends. It was so convenient: the vodka didn't smell on our breath, and orange juice and 7UP were things we always drank. Even better, nothing had prepared me for the tingling in my legs, the buzzing sensation in my head and the awesome feeling that I could do anything. I loved the feeling the drink created.

After that, Abby, Jo and I would go to one of our homes at noon a couple times a week. No one seemed to catch on that our lunch was a purely liquid diet. We often went to my house on Tuesdays, since my mom went curling that day and we were guaranteed to be alone. The kind of alcohol my parents had on hand varied, depending on how many cars my dad had sold that month or how many shifts my mom had gotten at the hair salon. One of our common drinks was what Abby, Jo and I referred to as "slough water." This was a combination of whatever alcohol we could access in my parents' liquor

46

cabinet without the drop in level being obvious in the bottles. We mixed the alcohol in the blender with ice cream and whatever juice was in the fridge. We were happiest when my parents had vodka or gin, since that was easily replaceable with water. Sometimes our concoctions tasted so bad we'd have to plug our noses to drink them. But the buzz was always worth it.

I'm not sure how it was that three girls in grade seven could be tipsy and sometimes drunk in class, and no one ever noticed. But then one day, when we were late getting back to school after a lunchtime excursion, we caught the attention of our teacher. He sent us to the principal's office. We were scared, but grateful that it was a vodka day so our breath wouldn't smell.

The principal, Mrs. Baxter, made us wait in her office for twenty minutes before she came in. I started to talk nervously while we were waiting. I wanted to make sure we were all on the same page with our story. But Abby cut me off.

"Shut up, Tilly," she said out of the corner of her mouth. "I bet they have this place bugged. I'll do all the talking. You two just go along with what I say."

Jo and I looked at each other, agreeing with our eyes to let Abby do her thing. She was a Bossy Boots Betty, and it was usually easier to let her do what she wanted. I was pretty sure they didn't have the office bugged. I thought Abby was being paranoid. But the longer we sat there, the more contagious her paranoia became. By the time Mrs. Baxter came in, we were terrified. The principal sat down behind her enormous desk, leaned back in her chair, clasped her hands in front of her and looked in turn at each of us. She seemed very, very scary.

"So, I've been noticing that you three have been leaving the school grounds quite often at lunchtime," she began. She looked again at each of us, then pulled a notepad and pen from her desk drawer.

Oh, no, this is it, I thought to myself. *We're so busted. I'm gonna get the belt for this one and be grounded forever.*

"I know you all live close by and are likely going home for lunch," Mrs. Baxter continued. None of us dared to exhale. "But I wondered if you might have any ideas about what the school could offer during lunch to make it more fun to stay here?"

I couldn't believe my ears. Jo and I waited for Abby to respond, but she didn't. Maybe she was in shock. Or maybe she wasn't as brave as she wanted us to think?

I began to stammer. "Um, it would be good if we could have more sports at lunch. There isn't anything to do if it isn't our grade's turn in the gym or on the field, so it gets boring. And the boys are always teasing us and won't leave us alone. We go home to one of our houses so we can get away from them."

This drew a hearty laugh from Mrs. Baxter, and I could feel my entire body relax.

I had hit my stride now. "It would be great, Mrs. Baxter," I said, "if we could have some organized activities for the boys and the girls, separately. Then we wouldn't have to go home at lunch."

There it was: the first time I lied to cover up my drinking.

And not to just anyone. I had lied to the principal, the person with the greatest amount of authority in my life after my parents. Facing Mrs. Baxter as a twelve-year-old girl should have scared me to death, or at least into telling the truth. But I had the opposite reaction. It was as if another part of my brain took over. The lie just flowed out of my mouth, and as it did, the feeling I experienced was similar to that of having a few drinks. My head was lighter. I felt warm and tingly. Perhaps the most frightening thing was that I felt invincible. I had just done something many kids could never imagine doing. I had lied to the principal and even given her suggestions on how she should run her school.

Getting away with that cover-up was the beginning of a long journey of stretching the truth. I would become an expert at that and at outright lying to cover up my drinking. My lying would cause me to lose more than one friendship and would severely affect my relationships with my family. After a while, no one knew what they could believe. Even I would lose track of what was true.

In the years to follow, my drinking would lead to humiliating situations, soul-shattering loneliness, one-night stands and suicidal fantasies. But for that grade seven girl in the principal's office, these were unimaginable consequences. All I knew that day was that my lie had saved our skins. As we left Mrs. Baxter's office, Abby and Jo looked at me with new respect.

CHAPTER 9

Auntie Pauline's News

I DIDN'T NOTICE IT RIGHT AWAY, but things changed in my family after we lost Grandma Tilly. She had been my compass, and without her, I felt lost. All of us were dealing with our grief as best we could. But sorrow ran deep, and our house became spookily quiet.

The only place I felt any lightness was on the ball field. I had tried out for and made the team that represented Kamloops at tournaments. It was a very competitive team, and I was grateful that with all our practices and games, I was out of the house a lot. It also seemed to bring a bit of joy to my parents and Auntie Pauline to come and watch my games.

One night late that spring, Auntie Pauline, Uncle Mike and my cousins came over to visit. As soon as they walked in the door, I knew something was wrong. My auntie barely looked at me, and she had brought a case of beer with her.

My dad must've known as well. He took a bag of chips out of the cupboard, and as he handed them to me, he put his hand on my shoulder, steering me towards the stairs. "Tilly, take these, and all you kids go downstairs to play. Don't come up until I tell you." Marie and my cousins had already raced down there, and I could hear them fighting over who got to play air hockey first. I took one last look back, and I noticed Mom was hugging Auntie Pauline.

After a bit of interrogation from me, my cousins spilled the beans: they were moving to Edmonton. Auntie Pauline had gotten a job teaching at a nursing school there. I was shocked. I'd thought my auntie loved her work in Kamloops as a psychiatric nurse. At least, she'd always talked about how much she enjoyed it.

"I know Grandma Tilly wouldn't approve of us moving to Edmonton," Auntie told me as she tucked me into bed that night. I was glad she still did it sometimes, even though I was no longer a little kid. "She always said, 'No matter where you go, there you are,' so I know she'd think I'm running away." She sighed deeply, and I could smell the alcohol on her breath. "But there are just too many reminders here, Tilly, of all her summer trips to visit us. I can't handle it anymore. I need a new start. We all do."

"But what about me, Auntie? I'm going to really miss you," I said, trying to control my tears.

"I'll miss you, too, my girl." She pulled me into a hug, and we stayed like that for a long time. "But just like Grandma Tilly, I'll always be with you in your heart. You can send me letters, and I promise to write back. And you can always call me collect. I'll show you how to do that before we move. We'll visit, too."

"But it won't be the same, Auntie."

51

"No, you're right. It won't be the same." She pushed my bangs out of my eyes and continued. "Sometimes change is a good thing, though. This is one of those times."

It didn't seem that way to me. How could change be a good thing when it was taking away the people I cared about most?

CHAPTER 10

Mrs. Murphy

THAT SUMMER WAS HARD. Auntie Pauline and her family had moved. I got my period for the first time, and my parents gave me the big talk about how now I was a woman and what that meant. I was mortified to have my dad there. All I wanted to do was call Grandma Tilly, and the reality that she was gone hit me again. My sadness engulfed me for days.

The only thing that made me feel better was marijuana. I'd discovered it earlier that summer with Abby. I loved how it made me feel. I thought I was more interesting stoned, and I was definitely more talkative. Marijuana was easy to get, and the little bit of money I made from babysitting helped pay for it. I smoked up a few times a week, usually with Abby. If she wasn't available, I'd go over to the park, sit in the swing and smoke up on my own.

Now high school was looming, and I had all kinds of emotions bubbling inside about it. I'd be in the same school as some of my friends from ball. But I felt intimidated by how big the school was and how many students there would be.

Would Abby, Jo and I still be able to go home at lunch and have our cocktails? I wasn't sure if we'd even get lunch at the same time. The whole thing made me nervous.

On the last day of summer vacation, Abby's older sister, Anna, suggested we go over to the high school to see if they had posted the homeroom lists yet. Anna was the expert we consulted on school and other aspects of teenage life.

"Oh, no, you have Mrs. Murphy for homeroom!"

The horror on Anna's face frightened me. Who was this Mrs. Murphy? And why was she to be feared?

Grade eight wasn't scary after all, and neither was Mrs. Murphy. She wasn't a popular teacher, but that was because she expected the best from her students and didn't tolerate any antics in her classroom. Once I got to know her, I actually thought she was kind of funny.

During our first week of school, Mrs. Murphy introduced us to Harry, a small goldfish who lived in a bowl at the back of the room. Each of us would take a weekly turn at feeding Harry, she informed us, so his life was in our hands. She'd had more than one goldfish go belly up in her years as a teacher, she said, and she made it clear she didn't want Harry added to that list.

The first month of high school turned out better than I could've imagined. I joined the field hockey team and instantly loved the sport. Just like with softball, I seemed to have a natural ability for it. Drama quickly became my favourite class. When I was acting, my shyness seemed to disappear, similar to when I drank or smoked up. I happily took on any role the teacher asked of me.

Abby, Jo and I had the same lunch break on Tuesdays and Fridays, which was perfect—I didn't have field hockey those days, so I was free to drink at our cocktail lunches.

I didn't get my turn to care for Harry until just before Christmas, and I noticed then he was in a different bowl. A much bigger one. When we came back from Christmas holidays, he was in an even larger bowl, and after spring break we returned to find Harry living in his very own aquarium. All of us had noticed the changes in the size of Harry's bowl, but until Mrs. Murphy pointed it out, few of us noticed that Harry himself had grown. After all, we were in grade eight and too busy noticing each other. But what she told us was amazing.

Goldfish grew as big as their environment would allow, Mrs. Murphy explained. When she asked us to take a good look at Harry, we oohed and aahed as if we were seeing him for the first time.

"He's way bigger," said one classmate.

"He must have taken 'roids over the break," said one of the jocks.

Mrs. Murphy laughed. "Actually, Harry didn't take steroids over spring break. Instead, every time I moved him into a bigger bowl, he grew." And each of us was exactly like Harry, she said. We would grow into whatever size of goldfish bowl we allowed ourselves to create.

"The more risks you consciously take to grow and learn, to try new things and have new experiences, the bigger your goldfish bowl will become," Mrs. Murphy said.

I didn't really know what she was talking about,

but a thrill of anticipation pulsed through my body nonetheless. It was like being up at bat when the bases were loaded. I knew I'd have to ask her what she meant by *consciously*, but not today. Not in front of the class.

CHAPTER 11

Moving Again

ONE AFTERNOON TOWARDS THE END of the school year, I came home from ball practice to find Mom watering the garden. I put my bike away, and as I got closer I noticed she was crying. "Mom, what's wrong?" I asked.

She turned away so I couldn't see her face and told me to go ask my dad. There was something in the way she said it that really scared me. Two students in my class had just had their parents divorce, and I was afraid that was what my dad was going to say. It had been a long time since I'd seen Mom and Dad hug or kiss, and from my room late at night I could hear them fighting.

I found Dad and Marie sitting at the kitchen table. They were working on a puzzle, like nothing was going on.

"Hey, there, Tilly, how was practice?" Dad asked.

"It was okay," I said. "Um, Dad, why's Mom out in the garden crying?"

"Come sit down, Tilly." He pulled a chair out beside him. When I looked at Marie, her eyes welled up with tears.

"I don't want to sit down. I want you to tell me what's going on."

"Okay," he said. "I got a promotion at work." He smiled broadly.

Something wasn't right. If he'd gotten a promotion and was so happy about it, then why were both my mom and my sister upset?

"Yes, and?" I said.

"And..." He paused, looked at Marie and took a deep breath. "And, we are moving to Nelson."

I slumped down on the chair he had pulled out. "Moving. Again?"

Without skipping a beat, he began his sales pitch. "I think you'll really like Nelson. There's a beautiful lake and lots to do for girls your age."

"I like Kamloops," I said, my voice shaking.

"I know you do, but this is a good opportunity for me. For all of us."

"It's not good for me!" I jumped up, and the chair toppled to the floor. "Do you ever think of us? Huh, Dad, do you?" I stormed out of the kitchen and headed outside to find Mom in the garden.

She put her arm around me and pulled me close. She knew there wasn't much she could say that would help. "At least we're not moving until the end of July, so you'll get to finish off the school year here."

"Whoopee. Big deal. Then what? We move to this town called Nelson. I bet they don't even have field hockey or ball or anything I like."

"We'll just have to find a way to make the best of it," Mom said. "I'll have to give up my job at the hair salon, my curling team and my ceramics class. So it isn't easy for me, either. But it's a good opportunity for your dad." She smiled at me, putting on a brave face. But I knew how she really felt.

Back in the house, I marched right past my dad and Marie and straight to the phone on the kitchen wall. I dialed Jo. *Please be home*, I said in my head.

She was, and I went over to hang out with her. Since her parents were out, we had free access to their liquor cabinet. Drinking was one way of escaping reality, and that afternoon escaping was all I wanted to do.

CHAPTER 12

Homeless

THE MOVE TO NELSON WAS A DISASTER, to say the least. We arrived at the beginning of August, "enough time to settle in and get ready for starting your new schools," as Dad had said to Marie and me. I was fourteen and going into grade nine. He had no clue how terrifying it was for me to start at a new school. Marie seemed to adjust more easily, maybe because she was more friendly and outgoing than I was.

On the drive to Nelson, my mom and I took the car, following Dad and Marie in our truck and camper. When we got there, I kept expecting him to pull into a neighbourhood, but we kept driving down a narrow road in the middle of nowhere.

"Where in God's name has your dad got us living this time?" Mom said. I sat quietly, feeling her anxiety rising.

Finally, we pulled into a campground. Dad came to a full stop at a site overlooking the lake. The view was spectacular, with the sun's rays dancing on the water. The sand had a few weeds in it, but overall it was a nice beach. We got out of our vehicles, and Dad said proudly, "Welcome to our home for the next few weeks. Isn't she a beauty?"

Mom's mouth dropped open and her shoulders slumped. "You're kidding, right?"

"No, hon. Our house won't be ready for a few weeks, so I got us the best camping spot in town."

He pointed towards the lake, putting his other arm around Mom's shoulder. She shrugged it off and went back to the car.

We ended up living at the campground for four weeks. Thank goodness we had bought a camper earlier that summer, because it rained almost every day. Mom, Marie and I spent a lot of time together, since Dad was working long hours. One of our favourite things to do was go to town. This usually involved a trip to the laundromat, where Mom showed us how to find a little extra spending money. We'd lift the lid of empty washing machines, unscrew the spinner in the middle and then lift it up. Underneath there was usually change that had fallen out of pockets. On average we'd find about five bucks, enough to buy us each an ice cream.

Our house ended up being nice, but it didn't really matter. Mom hated Nelson. I think it had to do with how lonely she was. She had no job, no friends and virtually no social life.

We only lasted in that house and in Nelson until the end of November. By that point, we'd had snow for five weeks, and Mom was done, in more ways than one. Mom, Marie and I moved back to Kamloops, and it took a long time for Mom to get back to being herself.

Dad stayed behind. "For work," he told Marie and me, but I wasn't convinced. I knew something was happening between my parents. It wasn't like they were fighting or yelling at each other. It was the opposite: they had stopped talking to each other. What terrified me most was that they no longer laughed or teased each other. There had always been so much lightheartedness between them, and now it was gone. I'd wake in the middle of the night in a cold sweat, out of breath and with the most intense pain in my chest, feeling like my heart was being torn into two. I never told my mom or dad about this, though. They already had enough to deal with, and they didn't need to be worried about me, too.

My dad came to Kamloops a few months later, when my ball team made it to the provincials. I was ecstatic. Not only did we win the tournament that year, but my dad was there to cheer me on. He stayed for a while after that, and our family was a family again. He didn't even sleep on the couch anymore.

But it didn't last long. Although Dad had physically returned to us, he never really returned in his heart. He loved us, but his feelings weren't strong enough to make him stay. Over the next year, he would come and go a few times, and he left for good when I was fifteen.

CHAPTER 13

Trouble at School

THE REST OF GRADE NINE was pretty much a writeoff for me. I had missed the field hockey season in Kamloops, and most of my favourite classes were already full, so I ended up in courses like shop, woodworking and careers. Mom was working two jobs to make ends meet and was never home during the day. That made it easy to go home at lunch to drink or smoke up. Sometimes Abby and Jo would join me. If not, I'd have my own little party. I'd often skip out on my afternoon classes, and near the end of the year that drew the attention of the principal, Mr. Peterson. When Mom was called in to a meeting with Mr. Peterson and me, she was furious. On our way home afterwards, she let me have it.

"Tilly, this is the last thing I need! I'm exhausted from working two jobs and doing everything for you and Marie. You need to sort out whatever's going on for you. I can't help you with that, so I'm going to ask the principal to send you to the school counsellor."

I felt awful, not only because I'd have to see the counsellor, but because I had let Mom down.

Luckily, there were only a few weeks of school left, so I only had a couple of appointments with the counsellor. All she wanted me to do was talk about my feelings, and all I wanted to do was avoid that. Most of the time I felt numb, except when I was drinking.

I continued to skip classes, but even if I stayed home from school for the afternoon, I always managed to be ready for ball in the evenings. A large glass of Coca-Cola was the trick; it perked me up and gave me the energy I needed. A new girl, Bette, had made our team, and we hit it off right away. She and her mom had just moved to Kamloops because her parents had divorced. Bette was easy to talk to. We laughed a lot and quickly became inseparable.

Finally grade nine was over. I was grateful that I passed despite my poor grades and my absenteeism.

I found a babysitting job for the summer and liked how it felt to get paid every two weeks. I also did a lot of running and practising in preparation for field hockey in the fall. Now that I had a job during the week, I drank only on the weekends. As a result, I felt good going into grade ten.

I had Mrs. Murphy for grade ten English and was doing really well until one day when a couple of friends and I shared a joint at lunch. My first class after lunch was English, and Mrs. Murphy knew instantly that I was high. I could tell by how she looked at me. Her gaze caught mine at one point, and she closed her eyes and shook her head. I was sure it was in disgust.

Once she had given the class our work for the afternoon, Mrs. Murphy came over to my desk. I slithered down in my seat, but she wasn't having any of that. She motioned for me to follow her to the hallway. I got up and went out, accompanied by the sneers and giggles of my classmates. I leaned against a locker, looked down at the linoleum floor and put my hands in my pockets. I was trying to act cool, as if Mrs. Murphy didn't scare me. Truth was, I was terrified. I liked Mrs. Murphy a lot, and I knew I had disappointed her.

"Look at me, Tilly."

Reluctantly, I raised my head.

"Why'd you do this?" she asked.

Her tone of disappointment was all too familiar to me. I'd heard it in many voices the year before. But from Mrs. Murphy it felt even more humiliating. Did she really want to know why I had come to class stoned? I thought, *I could give her a whole long list of reasons.*

Better not. Instead, I shrugged my shoulders.

Mrs. Murphy took a deep breath as she leaned back beside me on the lockers. I kept waiting for her to say something more, to send me to the principal's office or, even worse, the counsellor's office. She stayed quiet.

Shit. I wished she would say something. Her silence was freaking me out. After what seemed like hours, Mrs. Murphy finally turned her head to look at me.

"I really should be sending you down to Mr. Peterson's office, Tilly, but I'm not going to."

I hadn't realized I was holding my breath until it escaped from my lungs.

She continued, "I know you have a lot going on. I see it in that faraway look you have and in how your grades have dropped. But that doesn't make it okay to be doing drugs." She stood up straighter, no longer leaning against the locker. "I'm worried about you."

Worried about me? Mrs. Murphy was worried about me? No one else even seemed to notice me lately, let alone be worried. My eyes filled with tears, and it felt like someone was sitting on my chest.

Mrs. Murphy gently touched my arm. "Listen, I've been teaching for a long time, and I know when I have a special student in my class. You're one of them. So please, don't waste your future by doing drugs or whatever else you are up to these days. That path can lead you into serious trouble." She paused, as if waiting for me to picture the many forms that serious trouble could take.

"I see so much in you, Tilly. You have the ability to make the world a better place. But somehow you need to find a way to see all that good in yourself. *You* need to believe it. Lots of people can tell you how gifted you are, but until you truly believe it, their words will only be words."

She pulled a tissue out of her sleeve and handed it to me. By now, tears were rolling down my cheeks.

"As I said, I'm not going to send you to Mr. Peterson's over this. But I want you to check out the Indian student room. I think it would be a good place for you to hang out at lunch."

How did she know I was Indian? My olive skin and brown hair allowed me to blend in. Before I could ask her, she continued on. "And I need you to promise me you'll never

66

come to my class under the influence of drugs, or anything else, ever again."

I didn't have to think about it. "I promise."

"Now you go back into that classroom, and hold your head high," she said.

"Thank you, Mrs. Murphy," I muttered. As I reached for the door, she gave me a quick hug. I was too surprised to hug her back.

As we walked in, I felt my classmates' eyes on me. Everyone knew Mrs. Murphy's reputation, and I knew some of my friends would be scared for me. I wanted to shrink, but Mrs. Murphy's words echoed in my ears: "Hold your head high." I sat down at my desk, wishing I was invisible. I promised myself I would not disappoint Mrs. Murphy again.

I never did go back to her class stoned or drunk, and I checked out the Indian student room as she'd suggested. It became a safe place to hang out, somewhere I felt I fit in and could be myself. I was surprised at how quickly everyone accepted me and how easily I could relate to them. Mrs. Bell, the support staff for the room, reminded me of Grandma Tilly in how she moved, the stories she told and her way of making everyone feel special.

But over the next couple years, school continued to be hard for me, and our family life was painful. Dad visited infrequently and sent money even less often. Mom was still working two jobs, and I hardly ever saw her. I'd hear her crying in her room at night, but I was too scared to go in and comfort her. I felt helpless when she cried. I wanted to make her pain go away, but I didn't know how. Marie was caught up with her friends and school; she was always way more popular than I was. Like Mom, she was rarely home.

I was desperately lonely, and my drinking increased. I sometimes hung out with friends, but I never felt like I fit in, and I couldn't talk to anybody about what was going on for me. Bette was going out with a guy now, so she didn't have as much time for me.

And because I'd failed Algebra 11 after two attempts, I didn't have enough credits to graduate. I was devastated.

CHAPTER 14

A Visit from Grandma Tilly

I STAYED IN A DARK PLACE THAT SUMMER. I was too embarrassed to be around my friends, especially as the end of August came and many of them left for university. I had totally let my family down, too. I was grateful Grandma Tilly wasn't alive to see it.

I lived at home with Mom, Marie and my cousin Eddie. He had moved back to Kamloops to find a job and was staying with us. I worked as a waitress at a fancy restaurant and often got the closing shift. That provided a perfect opportunity to hang out after work with other staff and have a few drinks. Nobody seemed to care that I was underage. The thing was, though, those drinks were usually just the start for me. The night often ended with me at home, drinking alone in front of the TV.

During the Christmas holidays, Eddie took me to see the movie *Rain Man* and then out for nachos and pop. It was the first time in a very long time that I crawled into bed without having any alcohol that day.

That night, Grandma Tilly came to visit me in my dream time. In my dream, we were sitting by a lake. The lake was round, almost like a pond, but bigger. The air was crisp, and the leaves on the trees were gold, orange and red hues. The sweet smell of Grandma Tilly's pipe hung in the air like medicine for my soul. Oh, how I missed that smell. I wanted to hug her. But I was afraid she would disappear if I did, and the last thing I wanted was for her to go away again.

Then Grandma reached over and took my hand in hers.

"Tilly, it's time to start changin' your ways," she said, looking at me with eyes that saw through all my masks. "I know you've been feelin' lost, my girl, but you need to find your way. It's long enough you been out o' sorts."

"But Grandma, I miss you so much." My eyes filled with tears. "Nobody understands me like you do." All the tears I'd been holding in broke loose, and Grandma Tilly pulled me close, tucking me under her arm, just like she used to.

I finally pulled myself back and wiped the tears away with my sleeve.

Grandma Tilly smiled at me. "Li'l Tilly, you need to stop drinking that poison water. It's killin' you in more ways than one. And you need to go back to school. You're smarter than you think, just your ego's in the way right now." She gently took my chin in her hand. "I want you to figure out what you're going to do with your life. It doesn't matter what, but you need to do it with pride and dignity. Right now, that ain't happenin'."

70

I couldn't remember the last time I'd felt proud of myself or anything I had done.

"Look around here, Tilly." She lifted her head and gestured towards the lake. "I want you to remember the beauty of this place. One day you're going to come here and heal. This place is sacred, and when you're ready, the Ancestors will guide you here and help you."

I looked out over the lake, feeling I was seeing it with new eyes. The water was like glass as the sun shone brightly, reflecting the hills and exquisite colours of the trees.

Grandma Tilly rubbed my back gently. "I am with you every day, Tilly, watching over you. Whenever you need me, just close your eyes and you'll be able to feel me."

I looked at her, trying to etch the beauty of her face and the moment in my memory. I wanted to believe her. She had never let me down before. I woke up when my cat jumped up on the windowsill. The curtain stayed open, just enough to let the sun shine on my face.

My dream had given me a glimpse into the future, though I still wasn't sure what it would hold.

Dark Days

I DIDN'T STOP DRINKING after my dream about Grandma Tilly, but I did decide to go back to school. I had always dreamed of being a psychiatric nurse, like Auntie Pauline, but I never thought I could actually do it. I still wasn't convinced I could, but I knew now I at least had to try.

I started by registering in a grade twelve equivalency program at the local college. Now that I'd made my decision, I became a very determined student, and my grades were good. I'd begun to drift away from Abby and Jo, since they were busy with their jobs, but Bette and I spent a lot of time together. She'd become like a sister to me.

I was nineteen, and I had been drinking for seven years. By now I knew exactly the quota of drinks required to keep me in the happy zone, where things seemed relaxed and fun and I was still respectful of myself and others. Regardless, the seduction of an even better buzz from just one more drink often led me to cross the line. The person who emerged on the other side was arrogant, mean and promiscuous.

Sometimes I'd black out. Trying to piece together a night of blackout drinking was like watching a scratched DVD. The movie would play along nicely, and then it would hit a scratch and jump ahead to a new scene, with new characters and maybe a new location. Sometimes I did manage to reconstruct the events of the night before, only to find out it might have been better not to know. That's what happened on the night Bette and I went out to her friend Jeff's party.

I'd been working hard, and a night out to relieve the stress seemed like just what I needed. Bette and I started drinking at her place, with a couple of coolers to take the edge off. She had just moved downstairs into the basement suite of her mom's house, so we often spent time there.

By the time we left for the party, I was feeling good. Drinking always helped me to feel better about hanging out with Jeff and his friends. From some of their comments, it was clear they didn't consider me part of their group. I'd numb the sting of those remarks with alcohol.

Most of the guys at the party that night were football players, and soon we were all playing their jock drinking games. My competitive spirit and ability to guzzle beer made me the natural lead of the girls' team, and the games were on. But after the second round, I blacked out.

I woke up the next morning at Bette's place. I pulled on my Levis but couldn't find my shirt or bra. There was a football jersey crumpled on the floor beside me, so I put that on before slipping out of her place. I didn't want to wake Bette, and I needed fresh air desperately.

As I walked home, I tried to recall the evening. Everything

was clear until that second round…and then? As usual after a night of drinking, I felt sick to my stomach, but that morning I experienced more than just nausea. Something else was wrong, though I couldn't figure out what it was.

I spent the day in my room doing homework. I drank ginger ale and ate a box of saltines, but the nausea never subsided.

Monday morning was cold, dark and rainy. I was sitting as usual in a corner desk in English 101 when a girl named Sue, Jeff's girlfriend, walked over and stood by my desk. I sort of knew her from high school, though I wouldn't have called her a friend.

"Hey, Tilly, how's it going?" she asked.

"Good, thanks. You?"

"Yeah, I'm good. Hey, umm…" She sat down at the desk in front of me and turned to face me. "This is a bit awkward." She looked away as she played with the promise ring on her left hand. "Shit. This is hard."

The extra-sick feeling I'd had the day before was back.

Sue took a deep breath. "Did you know that some photos were taken of you at Jeff's party on Saturday night?"

The mere mention of the party made my stomach flip. *Photos? There were photos taken of me?* I swallowed hard, tasting bile.

"I thought you should have them." Sue placed an envelope on my desk and pushed it towards me. "I'm pretty sure these are the only ones. I took them from Jeff and then threw the negatives in the garbage so no more prints could be made."

I looked down at the envelope, frozen in time. I wanted to thank her, but nothing would come out. I couldn't get the message from my brain to my mouth.

The prof's loud voice as she came into the room startled me, and I jumped. "All right, class, open your textbooks to chapter five, and let's get started," she said over the chatter of the other students.

Even though I hadn't yet opened the envelope, I had a sense of what the photos were. I felt humiliated and ashamed. I picked the envelope up off my desk, jammed it into my backpack and opened my textbook.

After class, I walked and walked and walked, too afraid to stop and look at the photos. Finally, I ended up at Bette's house, using the key under the flowerpot to let myself in. I made a beeline for the fridge, hoping there'd be some coolers left from Saturday night. There were. I opened one and chugged as much of it as I could before the burning in my throat became too much. I swallowed a few times, then knocked back the rest. I opened another bottle, took a long drink and sat down. I pulled the envelope out of my backpack and placed it on the kitchen table. The white of the envelope looked stark against the dark wood.

When Bette got home, she found me on the bathroom floor, sobbing. The photos were spread out around me. She held me, wiping my tears away. Then she gathered up the photos and stuffed them back in the envelope. "I'm so sorry you had to see these." Her voice cracked. "I was going to tell you on Sunday, but you left before I woke up, and you didn't call me back when I phoned."

We sat quietly for a few minutes on the cold bathroom floor. It was Bette who finally broke the silence. "Tilly, I'm worried about you. I love you very much, but you need help. Your drinking, it's out of control—you're out of control."

When I finally got the courage to look at her, I was shocked to see she wasn't judging me. I was certainly judging myself.

I wanted to agree with Bette, but I was torn. I knew if I put it out there, there would be no going back. Even if I kept on drinking, nothing would be the same, because I had acknowledged I needed help. Deep in my heart, though, I knew that if I continued drinking, I would soon be dead. Either my drinking and driving would kill me, or I would take my own life—the pain was just too much.

"I need help," I heard myself say. "I need help." I collapsed into Bette's arms, sobbing.

After a while, Bette helped me up off the bathroom floor and moved me into the living room. Once I was settled in a comfortable chair, she made some mint tea and then called her mom's friend Bob. Bob had been sober and involved with Alcoholics Anonymous for many years. He came over that night and sat with us for hours. He offered to take me to an AA meeting. There was a lunch meeting the next day, he said. He would be happy to pick me up and take me along.

I told Bob I would call him, but I never did. I wasn't ready to acknowledge that I was an alcoholic. I thought I was too young to be going to AA. But my veil of denial had been slashed. While I continued to drink, the seed had been planted. Somehow my favourite beer didn't taste quite as good. The buzz was harder to reach, and my hangovers grew more vicious. My journey towards sobriety and a new life had begun, and the minutes, hours and days ahead would require more strength and resilience than I could ever have imagined I had.

CHAPTER 16

A Bigger Bowl

MY HARD WORK IN THE EQUIVALENCY PROGRAM paid off. When I'd completed the course, I was accepted into a psychiatric nursing program in Vancouver. I was both thrilled and terrified. It was exciting to be accepted, but scary to think I'd be moving away from home. I had four months to get used to the idea, however. I decided to keep working, and I also signed up for a chemistry course at the college. That would help decrease my course load once I moved.

On the first day of my chemistry class, I heard a familiar voice a few rows behind me. I turned around to see the smiling face of Mrs. Murphy, my old high school teacher.

During the break I made my way up to her. Before I knew what I was doing, I'd given her a big hug. "Mrs. Murphy, it's so good to see you."

"It's good to see you too, Tilly."

"What are you doing here in chemistry class? I thought you'd retired."

"Yes, I'm retired, but I'm not dead." She laughed. "My

husband isn't as healthy as he used to be, and we want to do more travelling. We still have so many places in the world we want to experience. The doctors told us we couldn't travel unless Fred is accompanied by a nurse, so I'm here to do my pre-nursing courses. In September I start nursing school."

"Wow," I said. That was all I could get out.

As we continued chatting, I glanced up at the blackboard. The chemistry equations there somehow seemed less intimidating now.

"Why are you taking this class?" Mrs. Murphy asked.

"In January, I start psychiatric nursing school down in Vancouver."

She raised her eyebrows.

"I know. Hard to believe, eh?"

"No, I'm just pleased for you. I always knew you were smart. You just had so much going on that got in your way. You got in your own way, too." She smiled. "I'm glad to see you've made some changes."

As she spoke, I thought back to our talk in the hallway four years earlier. I hadn't known the word *dignity* then, but that was how she'd treated me that day—with dignity.

"Are you still living with your mom, Tilly? If you are, I don't live far from your place. If you'd like a ride to class, I'd love a carpool partner."

"Umm, sure, thanks. That would be great." I felt a bit shy about accepting, but it would be wonderful not to have to catch the bus.

The following Thursday morning, I waited on our front step for her. The roar of a sports car's engine travelled up the cul-de-sac, and into view came a Mustang, candy apple red. The top was down, and the driver was Mrs. Murphy. My mouth fell open.

"Hop in," she yelled. "She's even more beautiful on the inside!" Her face was lit up with joy. This was a whole new side of my former teacher.

She reached across the front seat and opened the door for me. As I slid in, she said, "Tilly, meet Freda. Freda, meet Tilly."

"You named your car?" I asked.

"Sure did. I bought her brand new after my first year of teaching, and I've been the only driver, ever. Not even my son or husband has driven her. She has very low mileage because I used to walk to work every day."

I could feel the warm leather on my back as I fastened the seat belt. Once I was buckled in, we were off, the wind blowing in our hair.

"This is fun, Mrs. Murphy," I called over to her.

"Yes. But if we are going to continue carpooling like this, you'll need to call me Gayle."

"Okay, I'll try. It'll be a bit weird at first."

As we pulled up at a stoplight, I thought of something. "Mrs.—I mean, Gayle, do you remember what you told us about Harry? How people are like goldfish—the more risks we take, the bigger our bowl will be, and the more we'll grow?"

"I remember."

The wind in my hair was giving me a rare feeling of optimism. "I hope I have a really big bowl someday."

"You don't have to wait for someday. Your courage to go back and get your grade twelve equivalency, to come to college and then go off to nursing school...I'd say your bowl is pretty big already."

I wasn't sure of that, not yet. But I wanted to believe in Mrs. Murphy's perception of me.

CHAPTER 17

Nursing School

ON MY LAST NIGHT AT HOME, Mom and Marie threw a surprise party for me. Auntie Pauline had come out from Edmonton. Bette was there, too, along with a few friends I had made at college.

Auntie gave a toast that made me cry. "You are the first of Grandma Tilly's grandchildren to go to college. I know that, just like all of us, she's very proud of you, Tilly."

Being twenty years old, I wasn't sure I had the courage to move to the big city of Vancouver, let alone become a nurse. But I was determined to give it a try.

I lived alone for the first eight months of school. Even though I loved my courses and my shifts at the hospital, I was terribly lonely. I'd often invite classmates over to study and liked it best when my apartment was full. I was exuberant when Bette called to say she'd been accepted at university and was moving down to Vancouver herself. We found a fantastic basement suite and decorated it in a funky style. School and life seemed a whole lot easier with Bette there.

My drinking was still a problem, though. Two incidents in particular shook me up.

The first one occurred during my practicum at a hospital geriatrics ward. The night before had been the anniversary of Grandma Tilly's passing. That was always a hard time for me, and this year had been no exception. The vodka I'd turned to for solace hadn't helped.

I enjoyed caring for the elderly patients on the geriatrics unit, and I'd been doing so a couple days a week for the past three months. The morning started with getting patients up, washed and ready for breakfast. This included emptying bedpans and changing diapers for those who needed it. One of my patients was Mr. Stone, a well-known TV anchor who had recently had a stroke. His whole left side was paralyzed, and his speech was difficult to understand. Mr. Stone had lots of visitors, and he liked to be one of the first people up and dressed, so he could look good if anyone stopped by to have breakfast with him. He was a very proud man.

That morning, as I was getting Mr. Stone ready, a wave of nausea hit me hard. I barely made it to the bathroom sink before I threw up. I hadn't had time to close the door behind me. When the heaving stopped, I looked up, and there in the mirror, along with my reflection, was that of my nursing instructor.

I was about to conjure up a lie when she shook her head. "I live with an alcoholic, Tilly, so don't even try. Best if you just get your bag from the staff room and go home for the day. We can talk about this tomorrow, back at school."

As I gathered up my belongings in the staff room, I over-heard a couple of my classmates talking in the hall.

"Guess Tilly's got the flu, eh? She's gone home for the day," I heard one of them say.

"Yeah, the vodka flu," said the other. They laughed.

My backpack slipped out of my hand and landed on the floor. How did they know? Was it that obvious?

I was put on probation for the incident in Mr. Stone's room, but no one ever talked to me about why I was drinking so much. Since I was such a good student, my probation ended that term and it was as if nothing had ever happened.

The second incident came near the end of my second year of school, when my mom came down to help me pack up. In a few weeks I was moving back to Kamloops for my last term's practicum.

Mom had always been a hockey fan, and her favourite player was Wayne Gretzky. I'd been planning for months to surprise her with tickets to see the Vancouver Canucks play Gretzky and the Los Angeles Kings. As a single mom, she'd done so much for me and given up a great deal so Marie and I didn't have to go without. This was one way I could show my appreciation.

We went out for an early dinner so we'd be there in time to watch the pre-game skate. I had a few glasses of wine with the meal, then a couple of beers before the game started. By the time the third period got underway, I was drunk, and it wasn't long before I passed out in my seat.

I woke up to my mom jabbing me with her elbow. "Tilly. Tilly!" It took me a minute to get my bearings. Oh yeah, we were at the hockey game.

"Get up," Mom said to me. She was furious. "We're going to leave."

"No," I said, "the game's still on. I'm fine."

"You're not fine. You're a drunk and an embarrassment. Now get up and let's get the hell out of here." I knew better than to fight with her when she was this mad. She stood up to go, and I followed her lead. Other than that one time in high school when she told me to get my act together, she'd never really talked to me about my drinking. I'd always thought I'd managed to keep it under the radar, but now I realized she knew just how bad my drinking had become—after all, she'd called me a drunk.

That night, after we'd left, Wayne Gretzky completed his hat trick, and the Kings beat the Canucks 5–4.

My attempt to fulfill Mom's dream of seeing Wayne Gretzky had gone horribly wrong. I was beyond remorseful, and I couldn't look her in the eye for the rest of her visit.

CHAPTER 18

The Coyote

WHILE I WAS IN NURSING SCHOOL, I came up with a strategy that helped me get through challenging times. I'd close my eyes, take a deep breath and imagine myself in a graduation cap and gown walking across the stage to get my degree. I'd replay the image until I felt better and had the courage to carry on.

When I did graduate, walking across the stage to get my degree was just as I'd imagined it. It was my proudest moment. My parents, Marie, Bette and Auntie Pauline all came to Vancouver for the ceremony. It was the first time in years my parents had been in the same room, and I was grateful they were civil to each other.

After that weekend, I moved back to Kamloops and started working on the psych unit at the hospital. I lived at home with Mom and Marie. I was making good money for a twenty-two-year-old, which provided more opportunities to party. But I also started to save money, and after a few months I had enough for a down payment on a car. I bought myself a brand new Ford Festiva, cherry red with silver racing stripes down the side. It wasn't a sports car, but I drove it as if it was. I named my car Thelma, after the character in the movie *Thelma and Louise.*

On my next day off, I drove Thelma up the back road from Kamloops to Pritchard. It was the first warm spring day, and the sun was bright as the road unwound before me. There were piles of grey sludge along the sides of the road, once pristine white snow. Trees were starting to reveal their greenery, and the sweet smell of new growth hung in the air. I had all four windows down and the sunroof open.

"Hold On," a favourite song by Wilson Phillips, was blasting out of my speakers. The words resonated so deeply, I felt like they had been written for me. *No one can change your life, except for you* especially hit home that day.

I was speeding along, not paying much attention. Listening to the song over and over again had me pondering change when a coyote came out of nowhere and raced across the road in front of me. I slammed on my brakes and screeched to a stop in the middle of the road. From the roadside, the coyote looked back at me for a moment, then disappeared into the bush.

I pulled over to the side, my hands tight on the steering wheel, my heart beating like crazy and my head spinning.

It took a few minutes for my heart to slow down. Unexpectedly, a sense of peace came over me. I remembered something Grandma Tilly had told me: "When an animal crosses your path, it usually has a message for you." She'd told me the meanings of many animals, and I remembered her saying,

"When a coyote crosses your path, it means change is on the horizon."

I'd usually ignored the messages animals had sent me in the past. But today was different. Something had shifted in me, and I was ready to pay attention to the coyote.

CHAPTER 19

Bea

IF I WAS GOING TO STOP DRINKING, I knew I'd need serious help. I wasn't prepared to go to AA, at least not yet, but through my work at the hospital I'd learned about the services offered by the local Friendship Centre. I'd become more and more curious about my Native ancestry, so I thought this might be my chance to do both: get some counselling and learn something about my heritage. Before I could talk myself out of it, I called and made an appointment to see the alcohol and drug counsellor.

The counsellor's name was Bea. Short for Beatrice, I guessed correctly, but she set me straight on that at our first session. "Only people who ever called me Beatrice was the nuns at residential school. I don't have fond memories of them. So if you and me are gonna get along, you best be callin' me Bea."

Bea was a robust Ojibway woman who stood proudly at six feet tall. Her shoulder-length grey hair framed her beautiful green eyes and wire-rimmed glasses. Bea's fashion style was jeans, a T-shirt, moccasins and rings on almost every finger.

She always had a bag of knitting beside her, and she'd often knit during our sessions. If she got knitting really fast, you could hear her rings clanking together.

After each session, she would send me on my way with a hug. There was a lot of Bea to hug, and I loved that about her. Her personality and her zest for life would never have fit into a smaller package. Those hugs always put all the pieces of me back in their rightful places, shifting my turmoil into serenity.

At the end of our first session, Bea had given me a few instructions. "You need to go home and have a nap after our sessions together. And I want you to make sure you drink at least eight glasses of water a day."

"Eight glasses of water?" I asked. "I'm going to be peeing all day."

"That's what I want you to be doin'. Peeing out all those bad feelings, everything you been carrying that you don't need anymore. Water's one of our sacred medicines. It supports and connects all life, and it'll help you thrive, Tilly. You've done enough surviving. It's time to move on to thriving."

That was just one of many gems of wisdom Bea would share with me over our time together. She was a powerful healer. I came to crave her candour, her truthfulness and her teachings. Although there were times when Bea's honesty brought me to tears, I needed that, too. Our sessions were intense and filled with exploration. Bea helped me to be truthful with myself in ways I'd never been challenged to be before. With her, I felt like someone was seeing me for the first time.

Bea also understood the importance of culture in

recovery. She introduced me to Aboriginal teachings and values. I discovered I knew embarrassingly little about the true history of Aboriginal people in Canada. The little I'd learned in high school, I soon discovered, was mostly untrue. My sessions with Bea filled me with excitement—she was helping me to live the life my Ancestors had dreamed for me.

CHAPTER 20

Jessie

A FEW MONTHS INTO OUR SESSIONS, Bea sent me to my first AA meeting as an assignment. I asked Bette to come with me. She'd been to AA meetings with her mom, so she'd know what to do.

I was downstairs curling my hair when I heard her arrive. I hollered up to her that I'd be a moment.

"Where're you girls off to tonight?" I heard Mom ask.

I dropped the curling iron and bolted towards the stairs, but I was too late.

"We're going to an AA meeting," Bette said.

NOOOOOOOO, screamed a voice in my head. I didn't want anyone to know where Bette and I were going, and especially not my mom. What if I couldn't stop drinking? What if AA didn't work for me? She'd be disappointed in me again, and that I just couldn't handle.

"An AA meeting. Well, good for you two," my mom said to Bette.

I sat on the bottom stair listening to their conversation,

too ashamed to go up and face my mom. Finally Bette started down the stairs. "Hey, Til," she called. "We've gotta get going or we're gonna be late." When she saw me, she knew something was wrong. "What? What is it?"

"I didn't want my mom to know."

"Know what?"

"About the AA meeting."

"Well, you never told me that, so don't go getting all pissy. I know you're scared about going to the meeting. I'm sure everyone is the first time, but it'll be okay. Now come on, let's go."

We drove over there, but by now I was terrified. Once we'd parked outside the church where the meeting was, I refused to go in.

"It'll be okay, Tilly. Walking through the door is the hardest part."

I wasn't convinced, and I wasn't about to get out of the car. I crossed my arms to show my determination, and that's when I glanced in the rear-view mirror and saw him strut by. He was gorgeous—shoulder-length black hair, jean jacket, white T-shirt, faded Levis and cowboy boots. I'd always been a sucker for faded Levis and cowboy boots. I twisted in my seat to watch where he went. To my amazement, he went through the doors that led to the AA meeting. I suddenly felt much more interested in the meeting. I turned to Bette. "If they look like that in there, it can't be that bad."

She laughed. "Whatever it takes, Tilly."

Bette and I found the last two seats just as the meeting started. I kept my eyes glued to the floor. I was still trying to wrap my head around the fact that I was actually sitting in an AA meeting. But when I finally looked across the circle, there he was, my Indian version of James Dean.

He grinned at me.

After that, it was hard to pay attention to what people were saying in the meeting. I was consumed with this guy as we flirted across the room. When the meeting ended, he came straight over and introduced himself.

"Hi, my name's Jessie." He held out his hand.

I reached for it hesitantly, not wanting to appear too eager. "I'm Tilly."

I kept going back to AA because I wanted to see Jessie again, and in a few weeks we were a couple. Everyone warned me to be careful. The AA rule was no new relationship during your first year of sobriety. But the magnetism between us was too strong. I convinced myself that Jessie and I weren't like everyone else. We didn't need to wait a year to start our relationship.

I had an AA sponsor by now, and she tried to talk to me about "thirteenth stepping."

"Thirteenth stepping is when someone who has been involved in AA for a while hits on or starts a relationship with someone new to AA. In your first year, your focus is supposed to be on recovery. Starting a new relationship during this time is very dangerous."

It's funny what love can do to common sense and logic, though. Soon Jessie and I were together every waking hour. I even called in sick to work a few times so I could spend the day with him.

Jessie had been sober for thirteen years, he told me. I didn't hear his full story until we were on a hike one day. It was quite a climb, and both of us were sweating profusely. The path was narrow, covered with brush and twigs. I'd noticed Jessie was limping and was about to say something when he sat down on a boulder. "I need a break," he said, trying to catch his breath. "My leg is killing me."

"Did you pull a muscle?" I asked.

"Huh. I wish that's all it was." He rubbed his hand up and down his right thigh. "You know when we're out there, still drinking, I mean, and we sometimes do things we regret? You know how if we could turn back time we would, without a second thought?"

I nodded.

"Well, in one of my drunken states, I got in my truck and headed into town to buy more beer. Halfway there, I crossed the centre line and hit a car head on." He reached inside his shirt and pulled out a medicine pouch necklace, rubbing it between his fingers. "In that car was a family, parents and two small children." His voice grew softer. "They all died."

A chill ran through me. We sat quiet for a long time across from each other on the path, in our own worlds. Then Jessie started speaking again.

"I spent a year and a half in the hospital. They had to rebuild my right leg, and it took eight surgeries. At least I was alive. Or at least that's what everyone said to me. But I didn't agree. I would've done anything to have been the one who died and not that family." He looked across at me, as if testing my reaction. "My leg has never been the same. The only good thing that came out of all that was my sobriety. I haven't had a drink since that night."

I stood up, took a step across the path and wrapped my arms around him. My whirlwind romance with Jessie had become the centre of my life. I'd had infatuations in the past, but I'd never been in love. Never before had I felt this way about someone. It was all-encompassing.

I wanted to believe things were perfect, so there were odd things I decided to ignore, like where Jessie was on the nights he didn't answer his phone and wasn't at any of his local hangouts. "I was with a friend who needed help," he always said. If I asked who, he'd remind me, "AA is confidential, you know that." Then he'd pull me into a kiss and I'd quickly forget my concerns.

I was drunk on his attention.

CHAPTER 21

Indianition

BY THE TIME I QUIT DRINKING, I'd become dependent on alcohol in order to "show up" in the world. Alcohol was more than a crutch for me; it was my oxygen. I believed I needed it to survive. That was just one of many beliefs I had about myself that would need to change.

That horrible afternoon on Bette's bathroom floor, with the photos spread out around me, was the first of many times I would ask for help. But each time, the loneliness of the first days or weeks of not drinking had led me back to the pub or a cold beer and wine store. My relationship with Jessie didn't completely take away my loneliness, but it seemed to help.

Over that first year of sobriety, I had to learn a new way of living: how to be in the world without alcohol. Being sober affected my social life in ways I hadn't anticipated. I quickly found out who my true friends were and who'd been just a drinking mate. It was a painful realization, and Bette was one of the few old friends who stood by me. I'd started volunteering with the youth program at the Friendship

Centre, and I loved the time I spent listening to and hanging out with the youth there. I felt a responsibility to be a positive role model for them, and this gave me extra strength in my sobriety. But because Jessie was the centre of my attention, I made little time outside of my volunteering for anyone else.

Each year of sobriety in AA is celebrated with a cake, and I was excited to receive my one-year cake with my mom, Jessie and Bette cheering me on. The day after that meeting, I was in Bea's office for our weekly session.

"The chairperson opened the meeting last night by talking about the fact that we were given two ears and one mouth for a reason," I told Bea. "I'd heard that before, but somehow last night it hit home."

"That's because you were ready to take it in," she said. "And he's totally right, Tilly. We need to listen twice as much as we talk. The world sure would be a different place if we followed that a bit more." She sat quietly for a few moments, twiddling her thumbs. I'd seen her like this many times in our sessions, and I knew it meant she was considering something.

"Do you remember we talked a while ago about the importance of the number four in our traditional teachings?" she asked me.

"Sure, I do."

"Well, I think you're ready for the next level of that teaching."

I nodded, curious. I loved how Bea wove culture into our time together. With each teaching, ceremony and story she shared, I felt my pride in being Aboriginal grow.

Bea's face lit up. "I had my grandbabies sleep over last

night. I made them fry bread for breakfast. I wasn't sure why I'd brought the leftover pieces in to work, but now I know."

The first time she'd fed me during a session, Bea had told me, "This is our way, Tilly: to share teachings while eatin' or with tea. That way you don't just hear the teaching. Your body soaks it up, so it never leaves you. Someone explained it to me once—it's like we're feeding our spirit with knowledge and wisdom."

Her voice brought me back to the present. "Whaddya like on your fry bread?" she asked, getting up from her chair.

"Butter," I told her. "And salt, please." Everyone has their favourite way to eat fry bread, and that was mine.

Bea motioned with her head towards the table in the corner. "There's a fresh pot of tea. You pour us some while I go fix our bread."

I filled two mugs, set one on her desk and sat back comfortably in the big chair in her office. I took a sip. Ahh, sage.

Bea came back into the room, handed me my fry bread and closed the door behind her with her foot. Settling into her rocking chair, she took a bite. She had butter and saskatoon berry jam on hers.

"Mmm...this is some good fry bread, if I do say so myself." She smiled, then continued. "Do you remember from that earlier session how many chambers we have in our hearts?"

"Four," I responded.

"Right. And how many ears do we have again?"

"Two." I knew enough to be patient, since Bea often made her point through stories.

"So, two ears, but four chambers in our hearts. That's

because we need to be listening to our own hearts twice as much as we listen to what others have to say. Our heart, it tells us *our* truth. It's our guide for making decisions, for knowing our values, our beliefs and living a good life. It's one of the ways your Ancestors speak to you and guide you. I like to call it our Indianition." She popped her last bite of fry bread into her mouth and licked the jam off her thumb and forefinger.

I was puzzled. "Don't you mean *intuition*?"

"Naw, I like to think of it as Indianition." She grinned mischievously and gave me a nod of her head. "Well, we're almost done here for today. As usual, I want you to think about things, but not too much. Don't go gettin' yourself into analysis paralysis, Tilly."

"Aw, come on, Bea, I *like* analysis paralysis." I was teasing, but there was more than a hint of truth to what I said.

"I know you do. That's why I'm telling you not to go there." She rolled up her paper towel and tossed it into the garbage can. "Homework time."

"Ugh. Can't I have just one week without homework?"

The expression on her face told me no. "This week, your homework is to pay attention to your Indianition. Next time, I'm gonna ask you just how often you listened to those four chambers of your heart."

CHAPTER 22

The Medicine Wheel Teaching

IT WAS A GORGEOUS SUMMER DAY in Kamloops, hot enough to fry an egg on the sidewalk. I was on my way to my last session with Bea before heading east to Ontario for a two-week International Youth Gathering. I'd become more involved with my Native community, and I was thrilled when the Friendship Centre put my name forward to the gathering as a youth leader. The hospital had been generous in giving me a leave of absence. I didn't want to leave Jessie, but I felt I couldn't say no to this amazing opportunity.

It had been a couple of years since the conflict in Quebec between the town of Oka and the Mohawk people of Kanesatake. Tensions had erupted when the town decided to expand its nine-hole golf course to eighteen holes on sacred Kanesatake territory, including burial land. A standoff began, and as the events unfolded that summer, I'd watched with admiration the strength of the Mohawk people. Through

their courage, people worldwide were beginning to understand the needs of Native people in Canada. The events at
Oka had inspired a deep desire in me to learn more about
who I was. My sessions with Bea were instrumental in that
journey.

During this particular session, Bea decided it was time
to introduce me to the Medicine Wheel teaching. I'd heard
people refer to the Medicine Wheel, but I didn't know much
about it.

"Our Medicine Wheel is about who we are as human
beings," Bea explained. "We all have the same four areas on
our wheel: emotional, mental, spiritual and physical. No matter who you are, where you live, how smart you are or how
much money you've got, this is one of the few things in life
we share. We've all been blessed with gifts, and when our
wheel is balanced it helps us live our lives in a good way. We
feel happy."

It felt as if Bea was reminding me of something I'd known
all my life but had never been able to put words to.

"The wheel has many layers of teachings," she continued.
"When you're ready, someone'll come along and share more
with you. For now, let's start with this."

I sat up straighter and leaned forward in anticipation. I
wanted to know more.

Bea twirled her chair around so she was facing the altar
tucked away in the east corner of her office. "The east represents the beginning of creation," she'd told me on an earlier
visit. Her altar displayed items that were sacred and important
for Bea in her work: a smudge bowl, a braid of sweetgrass,

rocks, a small piece of rat root and an eagle feather.

When Bea turned back to face me, she had the eagle feather in her hand and was gently running her fingers up its sides. She stayed quiet for a few moments. Perhaps she was saying a prayer? It felt like forever as I sat there, trying to be patient. Finally, she spoke again.

"As I said, Tilly, we've all got the same four areas in our wheel. But how each of us balances those areas is different."

Bea smiled at the puzzled look on my face. "Hmm, let me think of a good way to explain this to you." She reached for the mug of tea on her desk and took a long sip. "The four areas of your wheel are similar to the four wheels on a car. If one area of your wheel is out of balance, it's like having low air in one tire. You can still drive, and sometimes you don't even notice the difference, but it's creating wear and tear on your car. That's just like us. If we're a little low on air, we can continue on pretty much as usual. But things will be a bit harder, life will be more exhausting and it'll take more energy to do things. And if you're really out of balance, it's like you've got a flat tire. Then you need to repair it as soon as possible. If you drive on a flat tire for even a short trip to the store, it can cause nasty damage to your car. For a person, if one of your areas is totally out of balance, it can really mess you up."

"What do you mean?" I asked.

"Well, that depends. If your flat tire is physical, and you don't take steps to balance it out, you can easily get sick. You might feel rundown most of the time, no fire in your belly, headaches. Stuff like that."

"What do you mean by 'fire in your belly'?" I thought I

knew, but I wanted to hear it in Bea's words.

"The fire in your belly is passion, what gets you out of bed every day, what gets you excited and willing to do what others aren't necessarily willing to do. And keep in mind that all four areas are interconnected. I know that's a big word, but I think you can handle it." She giggled, as if she'd just told a funny joke. "Let's say you have something really bad happening to you, or in your mind you see it as really bad. Your brain will react to this 'trauma'"—she used her fingers to put quotation marks around the word—"by releasing chemicals in your body."

This was the most I'd heard Bea say in one session, ever. I was eager to hear more.

"Now, I ain't a nurse or anything like that. But when I was doing my own healing from all the alcohol and drugs I used to try and stop the memories and pain from residential school, I had this shrink I saw. He was a bit of a brainiac." She looked at me over her glasses and laughed. "He's the one who told me the nasty things that had happened to me were 'traumas.' Whenever you remember those nasties, he said, your body reacts. I don't remember the names of the chemicals he mentioned or what exactly happens in the brain. I do know, though, it can feel like your heart is going to explode out of your chest, like you're gonna vibrate right out of your skin, and it's almost impossible to pay attention to anything." Bea ran her hand over the eagle feather and turned to place it back on the altar. "Whew. I've been talking for a long time, and I'm about done hearing my own voice. Bet you never thought I could talk so much, eh?" She giggled again, and her whole body shook.

I started to respond, but she silenced me with a swipe of her hand through the air between us. The motion reminded me of Grandma Tilly.

"Homework time," Bea smiled. "I want you to go to Ontario for the summer and be twenty-three years old. Go have fun and don't miss Jessie too much. He'll still be here when you get back."

Even the mention of Jessie's name made my heart ache. But Bea's voice cut into my ruminating. "It's a long time since I heard you talk about going out and having fun. It can be done without alcohol, you know."

I wasn't convinced. Hadn't I always needed alcohol to have fun and be charismatic and interesting? I felt a spark when I volunteered at the Friendship Centre, but other than that, I'd become dependent on Jessie to meet all my social needs. I knew it wasn't healthy, but I felt helpless to change it.

Bea's voice brought me back from my pity party. "When you get back from that gathering, we're gonna talk about you going to a cultural treatment centre. The time has come, Tilly."

My heart seemed to stop. I could feel my breath catch in my chest, and my thoughts jumped around.

Treatment?

Me, at twenty-three, in an alcohol and drug treatment centre?

What will my family think?

Where will my mom say I am when the neighbours ask?

What will come up at treatment?

Will I be able to deal with it?

I don't want to feel even more shame for not knowing my culture.

Again, Bea brought me back to reality: she'd seen the panic in my eyes. "Trust me, it's the right time for treatment. You're strong enough. But for now you need to have some fun—gotta get that wheel of yours balanced. Be safe on your trip, and pay attention to everyone who comes along your path. You never know who'll have a teaching or story for you...or who might need one. Be generous with your spirit. You're full of kindness; go on and share it."

CHAPTER 23

A Brief Connection

THE INTERNATIONAL YOUTH GATHERING gave me many opportunities to gain confidence. I was the only person from the Kamloops area, so I was forced to reach out and meet people. There were many times I felt like that little girl on the playground of a new school. Often I just wanted to hide, but I didn't. Instead, I tapped into some previously unknown strength and was able to make some friends. I was intrigued by everyone I met, and I loved listening to their stories about where they lived and what their lives were like in their home country. Luckily, one of the ground rules of the gathering was no alcohol, so that took away potential temptation or having to explain myself when others drank and I didn't.

Even so, I was lonely. I'd become more involved in my Native community, but I was still learning to be comfortable with my heritage. Although it felt right, and I stood taller as I shared my ancestry, I also felt like an imposter—a fake. Introducing myself as a Native woman brought up all of my issues about being mixed heritage. Native or white, white or

Native. Cree, Lakota or Scottish. Who was I? Did all people of mixed heritage go through such hell and confusion? Or only those of us who'd grown up in homes entrenched in denial? I'd learned from Bea about internalized racism—that happened when people who were targeted by racism started to believe the lies about themselves. I was shocked at how much of my family's and community's prejudice had seeped into me and my beliefs about myself, in spite of Grandma Tilly's efforts.

When the gathering ended, I decided to go to Toronto for a few days with some new friends before heading home. We bunked in at one of the youth hostels downtown. It was typical August weather for southern Ontario, the kind where your knees perspire and there's a constant drip of sweat down your back. We went to a Blue Jays game at the baseball stadium and wandered around exploring the Big Smoke: Toronto Island, the CN Tower, Yonge Street and Kensington Market.

On our last afternoon, we collapsed on the outdoor patio of a pub. My body ached with fatigue, and I was parched. I ordered a Diet Pepsi, passing on the ice-cold pints of beer that everyone else ordered, even though I knew beer would quench my thirst—and my loneliness—in ways that pop never could.

"I'm allergic to the stuff." That was the best response I could muster when my new friends asked why I wasn't drinking with them. I was pissed off at myself for being an alcoholic, though, and soon my crazy-making thinking kicked in. *Friggin' ridiculous, being an alcoholic at twenty-three. Maybe I'm not one, though. Maybe I just like to be dramatic and need attention. Maybe my drinking wasn't as bad as I thought it was, either. Maybe I could go back to drinking socially, just not when I'm alone. I was always the baby at AA meetings. What'd some of them say to me? They'd spilled more than I'd ever drunk.*

As I drew in a shaky breath, Bea's voice rang in my head. "Be careful out there, will ya? Remember HALT: don't get too hungry, angry, lonely or tired. Any of those'll put you at risk for relapsing."

Bea would cringe if she could see me right now, I thought. I was all of those things: hungry, angry, tired and most definitely lonely. How it was possible to feel such extreme loneliness in the biggest city in Canada? I craved a connection with someone: a true connection, where the person looked beyond all my insecurities and saw me for who I really was. This craving for connection made me miss Jessie and question why I stayed in Ontario for a few extra days instead of heading home to him.

My head spun, and my heart was racing. Was this what a panic attack felt like? The methodical beat of Billy Ray Cyrus's "Achy Breaky Heart" pounding out of the speakers didn't help.

Suddenly, I was ready to drown all these feelings in my medicine of choice. As I noticed the waitress heading towards our table, time seemed to slow down. It was as if there were two voices in my head, each critical in its own way.

The alcoholic voice began the debate. *You've been sober for over a year now, so you know you can do it. Just have a few drinks today. You can always stop again.*

My conscience, the voice of sobriety, took over. *Face it, you're a drunk. You can't have just one beer. That one beer will lead to many, and eventually you're going to wind up dead or killing someone.*

The alcoholic voice chimed in again. *You're still young. You've got lots of time to stop drinking. And you're in Toronto; no one will ever know.*

The voice of sobriety responded. *Don't do it. You've come too far to go back to that life. You might never return. Remember all the pain. Your pain, and the pain you caused others.*

I wanted them to shut up, these voices that were clashing in my head. The waitress was so close I could nearly smell her perfume. She gave me a quick wave of her hand, signalling she'd be at our table in a moment.

Shit! I needed a drink. *Come on already.* The alcoholic voice was proving more powerful. I slumped in my chair, crossed my arms and let out a sigh of exasperation. Then, out of the corner of my eye, I noticed two weathered brown hands resting on the railing that divided the pub from the sidewalk. I looked up. A man. His clothes were tattered, and they hung on his thin frame. But the dark pinstripe vest he wore suited him. From a previous life perhaps, or maybe just a good find at the local thrift store. Around his neck hung a buckskin necklace with a beaded medallion: a Medicine Wheel.

The man's eyes were almost black, and full of tenderness. He looked at me directly, as if he knew who I was...as if I was family. I felt warmth flood me. He leaned over the railing and said quietly, "Never question who you are or who your people are. It's in your eyes. I know it's in your heart." He gave me a nod of his head and a smile: a big, toothless smile.

"What can I get you?" The waitress's voice startled me back to the conversation at the table.

"Uh, can I have another Diet Pepsi, please?" I stumbled over my words, then sat up straighter in my chair. When I turned back towards the man, he was gone.

I stood up and looked up and down the street, but I couldn't see him anywhere.

I began to question myself. *Did that really just happen?*

My friends were still engaged in their discussions. Again Bea's voice and her wise words came to me. "Pay attention to everyone who comes along your path. You never know who'll have a teaching or story for you."

In the years to come, I would often replay my brief connection with that gentleman, remembering the warmth in his eyes and his message. The memory of his smile always calmed my spirit. That homeless man on Bay Street, I knew, had saved my life.

CHAPTER 24

Maisey

WHEN I GOT BACK TO KAMLOOPS, I knew it was time to deal with the reasons for my drinking. Bea was right: unless I uncovered what lay behind my addiction, I would surely find myself drinking again. As a friend later put it, I needed to slay my dragons.

I still had some money tucked away from my nursing job. I met with my supervisor at the hospital to explain my situation, and she extended my leave without pay for six months. That would give me the freedom to continue my healing. I'd be celebrating my twenty-fourth birthday away from Jessie and my family.

In September, when it was time for me to set out for the treatment centre, I asked Marie to take me. Bea had suggested early in our sessions that I go regularly to a sweat lodge ceremony, and Jessie and I had been to one almost every Sunday since. Marie got curious and started to come with us.

Since then, she and I had grown closer. Exploring our culture together had created a new bond between us.

I'd driven past the turnoff for the centre on many trips outside Kamloops and had always been intrigued by the sign that read "Culture Is Treatment." Over the next six weeks, I'd find out what that meant. We turned off the highway onto a narrow road, and after a few minutes a lovely round lake came into view. I stared at the lake as we drove along—I knew it. It was the lake Grandma Tilly showed me when she visited me in my dream. Her words came back to me. *One day you're going to come here and heal. This place is sacred, and when you're ready, the Ancestors will guide you here and help you.*

I said a silent "Thank you."

Marie parked the car in a clearing, and I went into a small office building to register. Before I knew it, I was hugging Marie goodbye.

"It'll be fine," she said, giving me an extra squeeze. "I'll be back in six weeks to pick you up."

She was just about to pull away when she rolled down the window. "Almost forgot this," she said, handing me a pouch of tobacco. "I heard it might be helpful when you're here." She smiled at me. "I know, I know, I'm learning." I knew what she meant—so was I. I waved goodbye, then set off to find my room.

I was just getting settled when there was a soft knock at the door. I turned to see a stunning Aboriginal woman entering the room. Holding out her hand, she said, "Hi, my name's Maisey. I'm going to be your roomie for the next six weeks."

Maisey glowed with zest and warmth. Her silver hair was cut

into a short bob. She had the funkiest glasses ever, cat's-eye style and solid white, setting off her beautiful brown complexion. Behind the glasses, her deep brown eyes twinkled. I could imagine her, as a little girl, being very mischievous. Maisey wore a black T-shirt tucked into her slightly faded jeans. They weren't the usual "grandma jeans," either. No, these were Calvin Kleins, and she wore them well. Around her neck hung a heart-shaped locket on a simple gold chain. Once I got to know her, she showed me the two photos she kept in there. "A photo of my granny," she told me, "to remind me of where I come from and who I am. And a photo of my first granddaughter, to remind me of the future and of how important it is to be a good role model."

Now, though, Maisey placed her suitcase on her bed.

"Welcome to our home away from home," I said.

"Yeah, looks like this place could use a little sprucin' up. Too much like residential school." With that, Maisey opened up her suitcase and began to unpack. She placed photograph after photograph around her side of the room: school photos, family photos, Christmas photos. She replaced the hospital-like blanket and pillow with a Star blanket and a pillow that read "World's Greatest Grandma." She unplugged the clock and the lamp on her bedside table, putting them in the closet. "Won't be needing those," she said. In their place she carefully laid out her smudge bowl, a couple of rocks and an eagle feather. She hung her clothes in the closet, and on the back of the bathroom door she hung a hot pink vanity bag. Finally, she zipped up her empty suitcase, tucked it under the bed and sat down on her bed with her back against the wall.

"There, now that's done. What'd you say your name was again? Sorry, but my memory ain't what it used to be."

"Tilly."

"Well, Tilly, what say you get a move on with your unpacking, and then you and me go check this place out? The lake is beautiful. The coffee sucks, the food is okay, but the lake is beautiful."

"I can do this later," I offered.

"No, no, you go ahead and unpack all your personals. Best to get set up so your spirit knows where it will be for the next six weeks. That is, if we make the full six weeks. You know what they say out there in our communities about this place, eh?"

"No," I answered. Did I want to know?

"It's supposed to be the toughest treatment centre in the country. Not many people want to come here, because they really make you work on your stuff. No just gettin' by or makin' excuses. No sugar, no caffeine, no visitors and no weekend passes until you've been here a month. We've got to exercise every day, go to AA meetings, do daily chores, go to sweat lodge twice a week and do lots and lots of circle time. You know, only about half the people here the first day are still here on the last day." She let loose a huge laugh and slapped her leg. "Geez, almost talked myself outta being here."

I was afraid to ask, but too curious not to. "How do you know so much about what happens here?"

Maisey ran her hand over the blanket she'd brought, tracing her fingers slowly along the outline of the star.

"I came here seven years ago with my husband. Both of us stayed sober after we left." She paused, and I saw tears dropping onto the blanket. "But last Christmas, he had a heart attack and passed over to the other side." She paused again, clearing her throat. "I lost my best friend and my husband of forty-four years that day. And it was just too much."

There was a box of tissues on my bedside table, and I passed it over to her. In the most dignified way I'd ever seen, Maisey wiped her tears away without smudging her makeup.

"Even though I knew it was the last thing he would've wanted, I started to drink again. I didn't know what else to do. I felt like I was going to choke on the lump in my throat, and the pain was unbearable; it felt like a bear was sitting on my chest. I hoped I was having a heart attack, too, so I could join Fred. The alcohol helped for a bit, but as soon as it wore off, there was the pain again. My Fred was gone. And no amount of alcohol was going to change that. So I knew I had to come back here."

She forced a smile. "Fred and I have nine children and thirty-six grandchildren, and I'm expecting my first great-grandchild next month. They all need me. And my community needs me. I'm one of our last language speakers and a band council member. So my time here isn't done yet."

I stood up, put my hands in my pockets and then took them out again. The posture seemed too nonchalant for what Maisey had just shared. I wanted to hug her or touch her shoulder, let her know I had heard her and felt for her. Instead I just sat on her bed next to her. "I think you're really brave, Maisey. I can't imagine how hard it has been for you or what it took for you to come back here to go into treatment again."

"Yeah, it's hard. I had to pass the room that Fred and I shared, and I almost left right then. But I could feel him pushing me down the hall. The truth is, it's a life-or-death decision. I knew if I continued to drink, I would soon be dead. Then who would be there to see our grandkids grow or to help our children make the most of their adult lives? The most difficult part was swallowing my pride and asking for help. I felt a lot of shame: shame that I had started drinking again, shame that my grandchildren were seeing me drunk, shame that I was breaking promises to myself and others. One day I couldn't even look myself in the eye in the mirror, and that was when I decided to come back here. This place...it's special." She smiled again, and I could feel the mood in our room lighten a bit.

I stood up and quickly finished unpacking, noticing how impersonal my side of the room looked. Besides my journal and a photo of my mom and sister, there was nothing that was "me." I wondered why I hadn't thought to pack more of what made me happy and comfortable. But it was symbolic, I realized. I didn't really *know* what made me happy. I'd become far removed from "me." But that was going to change. I could feel it, and I craved it.

There was hardly anybody around when Maisey and I set out to explore the treatment centre.

The main building had rooms for men on one side and for women and a few couples on the other, with the kitchen and dining room in the middle. Each half of the building had its own TV and games room. Maisey waited while I read the rules telling us what channels could be watched and when. Cable was available only on weekends. "Guess they think those fancy channels are going to corrupt our minds," she joked.

Maisey poured herself a cup of coffee in the dining room. "Guess it's this decaf stuff for the next six weeks. Sure am glad my son stopped in Vernon so I could have my last cup of full-throttle Timmy's." She lifted up the jar of honey and examined it. "This is for those of us who usually like sugar in our coffee." She spooned some in, stirred it around and took a sip. "Well, certainly ain't what I'm used to," she said, scrunching her lips up and shaking her head.

Once we'd left the main building, we walked towards the lake. It was a gorgeous day in the Okanagan, warm enough to get by without a jacket but with the feel of fall in the air. The trees were a symphony of colours, and the leaves that had already fallen crunched beneath our feet. We followed a trail and came to an opening at the lake where a sweat lodge had been built. Large blocks of wood and a few wooden benches created a semicircle around the firepit. There was such a sense of peace here I could feel my shoulders drop and the tension in my jaw fade away.

Maisey and I both knew we were on sacred ground. She was the first to break the silence as we settled on separate benches by the firepit. "Sittin' here like this, I feel I've come home again."

"I know what you mean," I said. "I go to the lodge almost every week back home, but it's different sitting here. I already feel emotional, so I wonder what it's going to be like when it's actually time for the sweat lodge ceremony."

"It'll be beautiful, that's what it will be. No matter what happens in there, the healing and cleansing is a beautiful thing. For many years, because I was forced to, I believed our traditional ways of doing things were bad. It took me a long time to unlearn that and get back to what my Elders had taught me. To tell you the truth, I think I'm still unlearning as we sit here. But I guess that's what life is about, eh? Learning…and unlearning."

We sat quietly for a minute, taking in the beauty and serenity. Then Maisey spoke again. "This is a magical place, Tilly, and I know we're both going to do good work here."

I was scared, but I was also ready. I needed to reconnect with my culture and with who I was as a Cree, Lakota and Scottish woman. And now I had Maisey to help me.

CHAPTER 25

A Sunrise Ceremony

THE SUN WASN'T UP YET. I figured I had about half an hour before it began to rise. I slipped into my Levis and a cozy turtleneck sweater, grabbed my bundle from my treatment centre dresser and headed off down to the lake, closing the door quietly to avoid waking Maisey.

I loved the walk down to the water. The leaves were falling faster now, and each day the crinkling sound beneath my feet grew louder. The faint smell of smoke from woodstoves and fireplaces was another sign of the changing season. That day I planned to gather some rosehips for Maisey. She made the most delicious tea with them. She had a secret ingredient, a medicine that grew only in her territory. And I knew that once she'd made tea, the stories that unfolded from her would transport me to another time and place.

As usual, I was the first one down at the shore. I unpacked my bundle, laying out my smudge bowl, eagle feather, sweetgrass, matches and drum on the red cloth. I knew the sun was about to come up over the mountain when the birds began singing, the frogs began croaking, and the energy in the air became electric. I smudged, saying my prayers and welcoming the day with a clean spirit and a clear mind. I picked up my drum and sang a sunrise song.

At first, I'd been grouchy and cynical about getting up at six to watch the sun rise. But I quickly realized how powerful it was to greet the day in a sacred way, from a grounded place and a place of thankfulness.

We'd been introduced to the Sunrise Ceremony on our third day of treatment. It started with Elder Sadie having us come together on the shore of the lake in a circle. "Today is a new day, a fresh start," she told us. "Each new day is full of hope and endless possibilities." She ran her left hand gently up the sides of the eagle feather she was holding. "It is up to us what we make of today and every day ahead of us. You are starting today in a good way, in ceremony." She pointed towards the mountain with the eagle feather. "When the sun peeks over the mountain and its rays dance on the lake, we will begin."

Indigenous peoples around the world have some form of ceremony that honours the rising sun and greets the new day, Sadie had informed us. As with so many of our ceremonies, there were different ways to do it, and she was going to share with us what she had been taught. Of the many teachings and protocols of the Sunrise Ceremony, she said, she was going to share the first level: smudging and prayer.

Elder Sadie nodded to the man beside her. "Frank will come around with the smudge, and each of you'll have a chance to smudge yourselves. He's using a mixture of sage and tobacco today. Maybe, for some of you, this is your first time smudging. There are lots of different ways to smudge, and you will figure out the best way for you. My dad explained it to me like this. When we get up in the morning we have a shower to cleanse our bodies. Smudging is like a spiritual shower—it cleanses our spirits. So when Frank comes and stands in front of you, he'll hold out the smudge bowl and the smoke will be flowing."

She handed the feather to Frank. "You can put your hands over the smoke, just as you would wash your hands at the sink," she said, demonstrating for us. "Then cup your hands and bring the smoke up over your head, asking for the ability to think positive thoughts. Next bring the smoke to your eyes, asking that you may see what you need to see today and that you see, too, the goodness and beauty in the world. Bring the smoke to your ears, so you may hear the messages you need to hear, and then to your mouth, so you may speak with integrity and kindness."

Each time she described a motion, Elder Sadie showed us what she meant. "Some folks also like to bring the smoke down each arm, asking for continued strength to feed their body well, and down the front of their legs, so they have the courage and strength to continue walking on the red road. If you would like Frank to smudge your back, please turn counter-clockwise, following your heart. When he is done, Frank will tap you on the head to let you know you can turn around. Continue to follow your heart and complete a full circle." She chuckled. "Some of you will find that if you don't follow your heart full circle, you may have a bit of an odd day.

But some of you, well, you are blessed as contrary people, and you will naturally want to turn to the right instead of the left. It's in your nature to go opposite to everyone else. I honour those of you who are contrary here. If this is you, just make sure you do a full circle. Once everyone has smudged, I will say a prayer, and our ceremony will be finished." She paused, and we could hear the birds singing. "The birds are telling us the sun is rising, and soon we will see the first shimmering of its light dance on the lake. It is time to begin our ceremony."

Since then, early morning had become my favourite time of day. I had always been a night owl. But now that I was in treatment, I was excited about life and the gifts that each day held for me.

I'd listened to Grandma Tilly singing her traditional songs, and sometimes they'd come to me just as I was falling asleep. I couldn't recall them at other times, though, or sing them myself. I dreamed of a day when this might change, when I would learn the songs I'd later sing to my own children. But for the time being, I resigned myself to repeatedly playing tapes in my Walkman in the evenings and learning that way.

As I sat by the shore, the sun warming my face and slowly burning off the mist above the water, I beat my drum softly to the rhythm of my heartbeat. I swayed gently from side to side, my eyes half closed. After a minute, I saw the shapes of Elders in the mist, two of them: a Grandma and a Grandpa. As they came toward me, I was in a place between the here and now and the other world, and I felt great serenity, tenderness and warmth envelop me.

The Grandma sat down beside me and tucked her legs

122

to one side, smoothing her skirt over them. Her grey hair was in a loose braid that fell down her back, tied up at the bottom with a piece of buckskin. Her cheekbones were high and pronounced, and her eyes a deep grey-green. She smiled as she brushed the hair from the side of my face and tucked it behind my ear.

"Hello, Tilly," she said. "We're so happy to see you and hear you sing. Your voice is getting stronger each day, just like you. This is a good place for you. When you get lost out there in the world, which you will, remember this place. Come back to it whenever you need to: all you have to do is close your eyes. Playing your drum will help, but it won't be necessary. Your mind is a powerful thing, you know. It can transport you anywhere you want to go; you just need to use your imagination and believe. Sometimes, when we are hurting, we forget to believe or to dream a different reality for ourselves. You need to remember to have fun, Tilly. Experience more joy! You have been taking life far too seriously. Lighten up, create joy for yourself. You will be surprised at what happens when you believe in yourself and the good in the world."

Next, the Grandpa sat down beside me. His smile lit up his round face, and the wrinkles around his mouth and eyes seemed to disappear. He had a small scar on his right cheek, and the longest eyelashes I had ever seen on a man. When he blinked, it was like the wings of a butterfly flapping. I could almost feel the flutter of air on my cheeks. His eyes were chocolate brown with the twinkle of a three-year-old boy, part mischievous and part old soul.

"Brought you some cedar, m'girl. Try addin' it to your rosehip tea. Nothing like it in the whole world. Way better tasting than that Diet Pepsi stuff you been drinking, and better for you, too. Now that you've stopped drinking alcohol, that poison water, you need to be taking better care of your body. You need to be disciplined about what you put into your precious self." He winked. "And this man you been thinking so much about: you need to spend more time thinking about you, not him." With that, Grandpa stood. He helped Grandma up, and they turned to walk away.

As I watched them fading into the mist, hand in hand, I wondered if I was dreaming. Had it been my imagination, or had it really happened? Had I just had a visit from my Ancestors? Was this the sacred place Grandma Tilly had told me about so long ago in my dream?

I opened my eyes fully and was about to stand up when I noticed a buckskin bag lying by my feet. I placed the drum on my lap and picked up the bag. Full of curiosity, I untied the top and reached my hand in. I pulled out a handful of what was inside: pieces of cedar.

CHAPTER 26

Family Photos

IT WASN'T UNTIL THE END OF THE FOURTH WEEK of treatment that I gained telephone privileges and could finally call Jessie. It was wonderful to hear his voice. I missed everything about him and could hardly wait for us to be together again.

Treatment changed me. I started to feel strong, and I was learning to understand and use the gifts I'd been blessed with. I felt deep pride in being a Cree and Lakota woman. I took this newfound power with me once treatment had ended.

And it was great to be back with Jessie. We picked up where we'd left off, talking and laughing for hours and going to the sweat lodge and AA meetings together. My mom and my sister adored him, even though he was fifteen years older than I was. I noticed that women were always drawn to his charm.

Once I'd made the smooth transition to being back in the world again, Jessie and I set off for an important occasion. Jessie's family had found out we were serious, and they wanted to host a feast to welcome me to the family. It took us two days to drive to his home community in northern British

Columbia. The closer we got, the more nauseated I felt. This surprised me. Was I just nervous about meeting Jessie's family, or was there something else going on? I tried not to entertain ideas of what that something else could be, but the possibility of being pregnant secretly thrilled me.

Jessie's mom, Molly, welcomed me with a huge bear hug. Usually she had a house full of family, she told me, but with everyone getting ready for the feast in our honour, and it being hunting season, too, she and I got to spend many hours together, just the two of us at her kitchen table. The woodstove warmed us. Both of us beaded, and as we did she told me stories about Jessie as a little boy and what life had been like on the reserve when she was growing up. I felt a powerful sense of peace, sitting at that table with her.

The day of the feast was a busy one for Jessie's family. But because he and I were the honoured guests, we had the morning and afternoon to ourselves. We took his family canoe out on the lake, and it was beautiful. It was early November by now, and most of the leaves had fallen. Jessie and I kept catching each other's eyes and smiling lovingly as we paddled along. It couldn't get any better than this, I thought to myself. Strangely, just as I did, a strong wave of nausea hit me. I thought I was going to have to hang my head over the side of the canoe. I recovered after a minute, though, and soon I'd forgotten all about it.

At the feast that evening, it was the crack and pop of the fire that I noticed first. I'd always loved the sweet smell of woodsmoke. Then the drumming began as we were welcomed into the Big House. The words Jessie's family spoke

126

in their welcome to me and their celebration of us as a couple were beautiful. I felt cherished.

Once the feasting had begun, however, I noticed a young girl talking to Jessie. She looked about eleven, and I was struck by how uncomfortable Jessie was during their conversation. He was agitated in a way I'd never seen. I knew something was amiss when our eyes connected across the Big House floor. Instead of giving me his usual wink, he quickly looked away.

The next morning, Molly and I were left alone when Jessie went off hunting with his brother. As I got the teapot out of the china cabinet, I noticed photos of some children tucked between the glass and the frame. There were shots of one boy and five girls, and one of them was the young girl who'd been talking to Jessie at the feast. Oddly, I hadn't noticed the photos before, though I'd been fetching and putting back this teapot for the last few days. How could I have missed them?

Back in the kitchen, I asked Jessie's mom, "Molly, who are the kids in the photos on the china cabinet?"

Molly turned away, looking out her front window towards the lake. I stood frozen, the teapot in my hand. Another wave of sickness hit me, and my head felt light.

Finally, she sighed. "Come, my dear, and sit with me."

I moved hesitantly towards the table. I wasn't in a hurry to hear whatever Molly was about to tell me. As I sat down, she took my hand. My hand looked so fragile cradled by hers, aged by arthritis and years of working in the garden, tanning hides and beading.

"I'll tell you right away, Tilly, you're not to marry my son.

He's no good for you." Molly glanced out the window again, choosing her words carefully. "There are bigger and better things for you in the world, and Jessie isn't part of that. Those are my grandchildren...Jessie's children. All six of them."

The fire in the woodstove popped loudly. Or was that my heart?

This time the nausea was powerful enough to send me rushing to the bathroom. After I'd thrown up, I stood to look in the mirror. The reflection looking back at me was not that of a pregnant woman, but of a woman whose intuition had been sending her warnings.

My body trembled, and I had to hold on to the sink to keep myself upright. I was too enraged to cry, furious with myself for ignoring all the signs I'd been given: the way Jessie would disappear and not explain where he'd been, the concerns shared by long-time AA folks who knew him. But I'd been too stubborn, too much in denial, too much in love. I'd chosen not to listen, and now here I was. I decided I'd pack my bags and leave as soon as I could. No matter what Jessie's excuses, and I knew he would have them, I needed to go home. But first I needed to confront him.

I splashed my face with cold water and wiped it dry. My pattern of avoiding conflict was about to be broken.

When Jessie got home from hunting late that evening, he found Molly and me sitting at the kitchen table. He stopped suddenly when he saw the photos of his children laid in front of us. His hand came up to his forehead, and then he turned on his heel and headed for the door.

Molly jumped up, her chair crashing onto the linoleum.

"Oh no you don't, my boy. You come back here this instant. You owe Tilly an explanation." Her voice softened. "Give her that respect. And give your children that respect. You need to deal with this, Jessie. Now, not later. You've been running all your life. It's time to stop. It's time to grow up."

She walked over to kiss him on the cheek, then turned him around to face me. "You two need to talk. I'll be in my room. Tilly, you come see me before you leave."

I nodded.

Jessie stood there for what seemed like an eternity. The fire crackling in the woodstove was the only sound in the room. I was determined not to break the silence. I'd always tried to make things easier for everyone, but not this time. I was at a crossroads, and I needed to make a clear statement that I wouldn't be treated this way.

Finally he opened his mouth. "I was going to tell you."

When I stood up to face him, my voice was loud. The strength of it surprised both of us.

"Really? When, Jessie? We've been together for almost two years. What were you waiting for? Until I was pregnant? Until we were married? You had many opportunities to tell me, but you chose not to. You're a coward!"

"Come on, Til, don't freak out on me here. It's not that big a deal." He pulled out a chair and collapsed into it, suddenly looking old. The lenses through which I saw him were changing.

"What do you mean, not a big deal?" I couldn't believe this man I was so in love with had such disregard for his children. "Jessie, you have kids. Six of them. How could you not tell me?"

"I don't know. It just never came up."

"How could it not come up? I thought you were the kind of man who would be proud of his children, not someone who hides them." My anger grew more powerful as I spoke. "Do you even know all their names?"

"Now you're being ridiculous. Of course I do."

"Don't make this about me. That girl at the feast, she just wanted her daddy's attention. You couldn't give that to her, could you? Not even for a few minutes. It always has to be about you, doesn't it, Jessie? You can't even use alcohol as an excuse for this one." There was so much more I wanted to say to him, but suddenly I needed to get out of there. Even with my rage, I didn't trust that when he turned on the charm I wouldn't get sucked in again.

Tears burned my eyes. "We're done, Jessie. I can't be with someone who hides the fact he has children, who won't even be a part of their lives. I can't be with someone who lies to me." What I said next stunned me. "I deserve better."

He started to protest, but I couldn't listen to another word he said. Something in me had snapped. At that moment I hated him, the man I had loved so much.

I went into the room Jessie and I had been sharing and grabbed my already packed bag. I had to move fast to maintain my resolve. I couldn't face his mom; I just couldn't do it. I walked right out of that house, with Jessie still sitting at the kitchen table.

I got into my car and started the long drive home, alone this time. Each kilometre took me farther away from the lies and closer to the truth. My truth.

CHAPTER 27

Cookie People

IT WAS A COLD FEBRUARY DAY, the kind where your nose hairs freeze as soon as you step outside. I was in Bea's office, sitting in her big comfy chair. "That's my Oprah chair," she'd once told me. It was three months since I'd broken up with Jessie. I was still grieving the loss of our relationship and all the hopes and dreams that had come to a crashing end. Even though I avoided AA out of fear I would see Jessie, I was able to maintain my sobriety, and I'd returned to my nursing job. Each shift provided opportunities for me to be grateful. Seeing other people's challenges and traumas put mine in perspective. I hadn't talked to Bea about Jessie much yet; my feelings were still too raw. But her teachings were a continual source of strength.

"Who was someone you looked up to as a kid?" Bea asked me now as she pulled her knitting out of her bag.

Auntie Pauline's face floated into my mind.

"You know, someone who believed in you? Maybe they didn't always like what you did or how you were living your life, but you felt better about yourself when you were with them."

The last thing Bea said confirmed it. Just the thought of Auntie made my whole body feel warmer.

"My Auntie Pauline," I said. "She was there for me when I was a kid, and she was the reason I went to nursing school. Washing dishes, shelling peas and helping in the kitchen never seemed like chores when I did them with Auntie. We'd be working away, and then she would launch into one of her amazing stories. If I hadn't known they were about the people she worked with, I wouldn't have believed they were true."

It wasn't until I did my first practicum on a psychiatric floor, I told Bea, that I realized just how extraordinary the people in Auntie's stories were. These were people who had lived through incredible adversity. Some of them came out the other side, but not always with their hearts or minds or spirits intact.

Bea was quiet for a few moments, leaving me space to be with my thoughts.

Before I began my sessions with her, I'd always found silence uncomfortable and done whatever I could to fill it. But I'd learned that silence was okay, even good at times. It didn't mean you weren't communicating.

The quiet allowed a memory to seep in. It was so clear, it was as if it had just happened, and the story came tumbling out. "I remember riding in the car with my auntie. I must've been about twelve. She'd picked me up from ball practice and was taking me out for something to eat. That was a huge treat for me. It was one of the times when money was really tight in our house. Next thing I knew, Auntie had pulled up at the entrance to a back alley. 'I just saw someone I know duck in here and I want to check on her. I'll be right back,' she told me. She jumped out of the car and disappeared into the dark alley."

While Auntie was gone, I told Bea, I played with the radio, tuning in to different stations. I was singing along to "Eye of the Tiger" when I heard the rolling of wheels on pavement. I looked up, and there was Auntie emerging from the alley with a woman who was pushing a baby stroller. There was no baby in the stroller, though. Instead, a couple of black garbage bags sat piled on top of each other.

"My auntie opened the door, and the woman got into the back seat. Auntie introduced us, then put the stroller in the trunk. When I turned around in my seat to say hi, the woman, Bonnie, offered me her first couple of fingers and her thumb to shake. She was dressed in layers of clothes, and she had a major case of bed-head going on." I paused as I recalled the scene. "Her eyes, Bea, they were so dark and sad. Almost like she was too sad to cry."

"I've seen eyes like that, Tilly. It's like if the tears were to start, they might never stop," Bea said softly, glancing up from her knitting. "Keep going with your story. I wanna hear more."

Auntie had started up the car, I told Bea, and as we drove she told Bonnie how my cousins had taken her to McDonald's to celebrate her fortieth birthday. "That was probably my favourite birthday ever," she said. Then Bonnie piped up from the back seat. "I used to go to McDonald's with my foster family for foster dad's payday and special occasions, and it was my foster mom's birthday last week." As she said that, her tone changed to match the sadness in her eyes.

"So how was it?" Auntie asked her.

"It was okay. You know, nice people, nice house, nice food. Everything was nice, nice, nice. But I just don't fit. Never have. My friends don't get how I grew up in a good home, with good people who loved me, never abused me, supported me through college, and now I live on the street. But shit, even though my foster family gave me everything, they couldn't give me myself. Does that make sense?"

My aunt nodded, and Bonnie talked some more.

"I was Native and they weren't, and that bridge was one we could never find our way over. Same thing happened in college. I was the only Native in so many of my classes, and them profs, well, they always wanted me to speak on behalf of Natives, like I was the voice for all of us or something. But I didn't have anything Native, Pauline. I had the skin colour of an Indian, but I knew nothing of who my people were, my culture or my language. Or even where I was from. All I knew was I didn't fit in the white world, and I don't fit in the Native world either. The only place I fit is on the street, where no one expects anything of me and I can just be Bonnie—not Bonnie the Native girl or Bonnie the foster daughter, just Bonnie. Or 'Bobby Bon,' as they call me out there."

I shifted my position in the big chair, which brought me back to Bea's office. "My judgments about people living on the street began to change that night. You know, I still see Bonnie every now and then when I'm downtown. Somehow

134

she found out I work on the psych unit at the hospital, and she teases me about following in my auntie's footsteps."

Bea chimed in. "Sounds like your auntie taught you some good life lessons. People connect the same way all around the world, Native and non-Native: through our stories and experiences."

She set her knitting needles down in her lap. "When I did my counselling training, they kept talkin' about how to build relationships through trust and this thing they called rapport. It was fancy words for how we've always done things as Indian people—connecting through stories and teachings. That's what all our cultures are about. That gives us our roots. And when we don't have our roots firmly in the ground, we get blown all over the place."

I took a sip of my tea, now gone cold from all my reminiscing. I'd never thought of it like that before. My auntie had always been important in my life, but I'd never appreciated how much she'd influenced me. She always seemed to know when I needed a hug, a game of crib or one of her special cinnamon buns. "I could tell Auntie anything, Bea, and I never felt like she judged me. When I was still drinking, I'd phone her in Edmonton and tell her some pretty shameful things. She was the first to give me a kick in the butt if I was getting myself into trouble. Not an actual one, but she was very strict on respect: self-respect and respecting others. No matter what I'd done, I always knew I could go to Auntie. She'd ask me what I'd learned from the situation and what I'd do differently next time. She never allowed me to wallow in self-pity for long."

Bea picked up her knitting again. "That's what I mean. These special people in our lives, they don't always like our behaviour, but they love us, and they see what we *could* be. They see the gifts the Creator has given us, and they're always encouraging us to discover and use them. My Nokomis— that's Grandma in my language—used to call them Cookie People."

"Cookie People?"

"Sure. Those people in our lives are like cookies to our spirit. When we are around 'em, we feel good about ourselves."

I nodded. This made sense to me.

Bea continued, "I remember so clearly sittin' by the fire with my Nokomis while she told us to find our Cookie People and hold 'em close. They'd been put in our path to help us see our true beauty, she said." She smiled. "My Nokomis was a Cookie Person for me."

I smiled, too. It was almost a year since I'd travelled to Edmonton for Auntie Pauline's retirement party. She'd be in Kamloops this summer for a golfing holiday, I knew, and I was looking forward to that. Especially now, I felt like I needed to be in her presence.

Bea's voice brought me back to reality. "I hope you remember when you have children that they need Cookie People in their lives. Parents are often Cookie People for their children, or at least until those kids become teenagers." She laughed.

"Yeah, no way my mom could have been a Cookie Person for me then," I said. I thought about all I'd put my mom through. It must have been so hard for her as a single parent, with no one to share the load.

136

It was as if Bea could hear my thoughts. "No child was meant to be raised by just their parents. Everyone in the family has a role in the raisin' up of children. That's how it used to be, before things got all messed up in our families. Lots of us are workin' hard to get back to that traditional way."

Bea slipped her knitting needles and yarn back in their bag. "It's time for your homework, Tilly. Two things this week."

"Two?" I moaned.

"Be careful, or I'll give you three." She slid her glasses up the brow of her nose and raised her eyebrows at me. I knew she wasn't kidding.

"The first thing I want you to do is write a letter of gratitude to your Auntie Pauline and any other Cookie People in your life. I want you to mail those before we see each other next week. If you write one to your Grandma Tilly, then next time you go to the sweat you can put it in the fire at the end of the ceremony."

I nodded, already thinking of what I might say.

Bea reached into her desk drawer and handed me a blank notebook. "This here is your Gratitude Journal. Each night before you go to sleep, I want you to make a list of ten things or people you're grateful for."

"Ten?" I asked. It seemed overwhelming.

"Yes, ten. If you do it before bed, you'll fall asleep in good spirits. This will help the Ancestors guide you through your dream time." Before I could ask any questions, Bea stood up. "That's it for today. Come on over here and give me a hug, and then off ya go."

CHAPTER 28

A Healing Session

BEA'S OFFICE WAS A SANCTUARY FOR ME, a place where extraordinary healing happened. There was something so powerful about my sessions with her, and today I'd decided it was time to talk about Jessie. She knew part of the story already, but I needed to tell it again.

"It was at my first AA meeting, remember, the one you sent me to as homework?"

She nodded.

"I still remember how Jessie looked in the rear-view mirror as he strutted by. He had the most caressable butt I'd ever seen on an Indian man—no bannock butt there."

That made Bea laugh. "Most of our men have flat butts, but I never heard 'em called bannock butts before. That's a good one."

"I know now I should have listened to everyone and waited until I was at least a year sober before dating, but I convinced myself that Jessie and I weren't like everyone else." I was quiet for a few moments as I reflected on how crazy my thinking had been.

As usual, Bea had a good sense of what was going on in my head. "So what made you think your relationship would be different?"

"I don't know. I guess I just thought what we had was so special that we could rise above any challenges that might come along. I was happier than I had ever been. And as you know, my family loved him, even if he was fifteen years older than me and carried a fair chunk of baggage. Actually, it turned out his baggage could have filled a U-Haul trailer." It felt good to laugh.

"Tell me more," Bea said.

"Well, as you know, he was quite a ladies' man. Wherever we went, there were always women he knew. I never asked about them, mostly because I didn't want to know. That should have been a clue for me, but I was too far gone to pay attention." It was hard not to beat myself up for ignoring all the signs that I'd been given along the way. When I looked back, the messages were everywhere. "He was a wounded little boy in a grown man's body, Bea."

As always, I couldn't help thinking about the family Jessie had killed and the friends and relatives who'd been left behind. I was grateful I'd made it home safely the many, many times I'd driven drunk myself. Perhaps witnessing the pain Jessie lived with had been a gift to me.

"Keep talking," Bea urged me.

As I shared the story again, it was like I was there, reliving it. I felt sick as I recalled how Molly had taken my hand in hers when she told me the children in the photos were Jessie's. How when I'd confronted Jessie and asked why he hadn't told me, his response was that it had never come up. And how I'd shocked myself by telling him I deserved better.

I sat there with my heart breaking in two all over again.

Eventually, Bea's voice brought me back from the nightmare. "Whenever you're ready, Tilly, there's the smudge bowl and a glass of water beside you. Take your time, though. It'll take a bit of time for your spirit to come back to this room."

Slowly, I began to be aware of sweetgrass burning. I sat with my eyes closed, breathing in the healing medicine. I said a silent prayer, grateful I'd had the strength to leave Jessie and not return to the relationship, even though I still missed him desperately some days.

I lifted the braid of sweetgrass and smudged myself, then drank the whole glass of water. Bea stood up and refilled it, indicating I should drink the second glass, too. Thanks to her, I'd come to know the healing powers of water.

"Whew, that was some powerful work you just did there." Bea smiled. "Now it's time for you to go home and have a nap. Keep drinking lots of water today, and write about anything more that comes up for you."

She extended her hand to help me up from my chair. She hugged me a little longer than usual, and when she pulled back she held my face in her hands. "You did real good here today. Be proud of yourself." Her smile reminded me of Grandma Tilly's.

CHAPTER 29

Our Children Remember

AS I CONTINUED TO HEAL from my relationship with Jessie, I needed consistency and routine. I lived with my mom and Marie and kept working at the hospital, seeing Bea weekly and going to ceremony. I'd found a new sweat lodge to go to and I still avoided AA; I wasn't sure I'd have the strength to walk away from Jessie again. But as spring rolled around, I realized I was ready to be more social again. I wanted to do something that made me feel good, so I joined an all-Native women's ball team.

I hit it off right away with our coach, Mabel. Perhaps it was because we worked in similar fields, or because our first ball practice took the form of a sharing circle as a way to get to know each other. Mabel was a counsellor and also ran groups for people in recovery from addictions: alcohol, drugs, sex, food, bingo. "You name it, I've dealt with it in my groups," she told me.

At our end-of-season team party in July, Mabel came over and sat down beside me.

I was glad to have a moment alone with her. "Thanks for everything this season," I said. "I'd forgotten how much I loved playing ball, and you helped me remember. You got me back in shape, too." I lifted my sleeve and showed her my muscle with a big grin on my face.

"Yeah, that part of it was hard work," Mabel said, with a hint of sarcasm. "Actually, I've got a proposition for you."

She's going to ask me to help her coach a girl's team, I guessed. But I couldn't have been more wrong.

"I've been watching you, how the team members talk to you when they've got stuff going on," Mabel said. "You have a way of listening that makes people feel special. I bet you're a good nurse up there at the hospital."

I tipped my head a bit to the side.

"I know, you're too humble to agree." Mabel took a sip of her pop and continued. "I've got contracts next month to do healing workshops in a few of our communities in B.C. and Saskatchewan. What do you think? You interested in coming along and being my helper?" She grinned like a coach who knows her players well and has just challenged one of them to be bigger than she thinks she can be.

"No need to answer me just yet. Think about it and get back to me." She stood up to rejoin the party. "Sure would love to have you along, though. We could do powerful work together."

I was intrigued by Mabel's invitation. She often joked that at fifty-five years old she was an Elder in training. To my mind, she was already an Elder, and her life had been training enough.

In the sharing circle at our first practice, she'd told us her parents had died in a house fire when she was little. She and her brother had been raised by their grandparents, Indian day-school survivors who'd been helpless to prevent their own children from being taken away to residential school. They vowed it wouldn't happen to another generation, so the summer Mabel turned five, her grandparents had moved high into the mountains, hiding Mabel and her brother from the Indian agents.

Mabel had grown up with the land as her school. As well as teaching her to read and write, her grandma had taught her about all the medicines that grew in their territory, how to harvest them and how to use them for different ailments. Mabel became famous in Indian country for being able to bead anything you wanted on a pair of moccasins. By the time I met her, her beaded jackets sold for hundreds of dollars.

I still loved my work at the hospital, but I was frustrated with the increasing use of medication for patients. Many of them needed other kinds of tools to help them through, and I knew from personal experience how important it was to have a guide through the healing process. My *Indianition* was telling me it was time to try a new way of working. A few days later, I called Mabel and told her I'd love to be her helper for the rest of the summer.

I soon discovered that Mabel was an extraordinary healer. She was also a Pipe Carrier, and the evening before each of our sessions started, the two of us would have a pipe ceremony. She said it was important to invite the Ancestors on whose land we were guests to help with the work to be done.

Sometimes she'd hold a pipe ceremony with the participants, too, and it was during one of those that I first witnessed the magic of our children remembering.

That week we were in a remote First Nations community in northern British Columbia. As we brought the day to completion and prepared for our closing circle, Mabel announced that, because of the full moon, she'd be having a special pipe ceremony, and anyone who'd like to come was welcome.

"Everyone must come clean and sober," she told us. "We'll make a sacred space for women who are having their moon time to participate. Our power is stronger then, and our dreams are more powerful, too. That can influence others."

Mabel's announcement created a great deal of discussion. The people in that community knew the pipe was part of their ways, but the federal government had outlawed it along with other First Nations ceremonies between 1885 and 1951. Although some people had continued to practise ceremonies in secret, keeping them alive, many ceremonies had not been practised or passed on. It was as if they had been put to sleep. But they had not disappeared. They were simply waiting to be awoken by a new generation who could breathe life and vibrancy into them again.

That evening, as Mabel and I walked to the ceremony, the air was cool and crisp. The smell of woodsmoke lingered in the air. Eighteen people from the small community were already at the health centre waiting for us, a remarkable testimony to their desire to be reminded of their traditions.

"All right, everyone, have a seat in the circle and let's get started," Mabel said. I sat across the circle from her and removed my drum and stick from my drum bag. Gently, I rubbed my hand in a circular motion on my drum to warm it up.

Once everyone was seated on the floor, Mabel asked if anyone had ever been to a pipe ceremony before. No one had. Although there was a heavy feeling in the circle as people realized their loss, there was also hope. That night was a new chapter, a chance to sit in ceremony and start to learn the ways and teachings of the pipe.

"Let's go over what's gonna happen tonight," Mabel began. "Tilly will come around in a minute with the smudge. Once everyone has smudged, she'll sing a prayer song. As she sings, I'll be offering prayers and blessing the tobacco. Then I'll load the pipe with the tobacco and we'll pass it around the circle. Each of you will have an opportunity to smoke it. If you don't want to smoke it, you don't have to. You can simply say "All my relations" and pass it to the next person. This tobacco isn't like the kind in cigarettes—that has a lot of chemicals. The way we use cigarettes now isn't the way our people used tobacco in the old days, either. Many consider it a gift from the Creator, so it's not to be misused. The tobacco I have tonight comes from a Haudenosaunee friend of mine. It has some kinnikinnick in it, too."

The little girl on Mabel's left raised her hand. Mabel smiled at her fondly. "It's okay, honey, this isn't school, so you don't need to raise your hand." The group chuckled. "What is it?"

"Umm…" The girl lifted her shoulders shyly and looked over at her mom, who gave her a reassuring smile. "What's kinnikinnickinikini?"

"Thanks for asking that question. You know, I grew up mixing kinnikinnick for my grandparents' pipes, so I forget that not everyone knows what it is. This mix includes the bark from red willow trees and leaves from raspberry plants. Sometimes kinnikinnick has other leaves in it, too." Mabel gave the young girl a wink, then turned back to the circle. "When the pipe has gone full circle, I'll smoke it until the tobacco is finished. Once that's done, we'll have a sharing circle and then share the food you've all brought."

After I'd smudged everyone in the circle, I sang the prayer song Mabel had taught me, while she unwrapped the bundle in front of her, placing a piece of red cloth down first and then her pouch of tobacco. Next she removed the pipe stem and bowl from her buckskin bag and smudged them. As she said her prayers and loaded the pipe with tobacco, I continued to sing, noticing how with each of the four rounds of the song, everyone relaxed a bit more.

Usually when I finished the prayer song, Mabel would light her pipe, smoke it and then pass it along to the person to her left. That evening, she was guided to do the ceremony a little differently. After lighting the pipe, instead of smoking it, she passed it to the young girl who had asked about kinnikinnick.

The girl held the bowl of the pipe in her left hand and the stem in her right. She brought it to her lips, stroked the stem as she inhaled and then released the smoke. She used her right hand to guide the smoke up to the spirit world. She took another puff, released the smoke and used her hand to guide the smoke down to Mother Earth. She continued these actions, guiding smoke towards the centre of the circle and then to all four directions. After she had finished smoking the pipe, she held it to her heart and, with her eyes closed and tiny lips gently moving, said her prayers. She then turned the pipe full circle and handed it to her mom.

We had just witnessed something extraordinary. I was covered in goosebumps. How had that girl known exactly what to do? We were seeing the once-forgotten pipe ceremony come to life, and a young girl was showing her community the way.

Once the pipe had gone around the circle and all the tobacco was smoked, Mabel took the pipe apart and returned it to her bundle. She spoke a few words about the importance of gratitude and invited each participant to share two things they were grateful for. She closed the ceremony with a prayer. Then it was time to feast on the food everyone had brought.

Later that evening, Mabel explained to me about body memory. "Many people believe that at some level we remember the experiences of our Ancestors," she said. "This includes the traumas they may have endured, as well as their ceremonies, songs and languages. Our children remember. We just have to make the space for them to do that—and perhaps for us to remember as well. That's what we saw tonight. We made space by offering the ceremony, and that young girl remembered. She remembered how to hold the pipe, how to smoke it and how to offer the smoke." Mabel smiled, and I smiled back. We both knew what had happened that night was profound.

CHAPTER 30

The Honour Song

AFTER MY WORK WITH MABEL THAT AUGUST, I got a job
setting up a youth suicide prevention program in Kamloops.
I loved the work, which required me to do workshops in high
schools and reserve communities. I was three years sober by
then, and feeling solid in my recovery. That is, until one
Saturday at a Pow Wow when I saw Jessie again. I wasn't prepared for the impact he had on me.

So there I was at eight thirty the following Monday morning, waiting for the Friendship Centre to open so I could call
and get an appointment with Bea. I hadn't had any sessions
with her for a few months; she'd sent me away to work on
things on my own. But now I needed to see her.

"Let me check Bea's calendar, but I think she is booked
solid this week," the receptionist said. I waited anxiously while
she put me on hold. I didn't think I could wait a week. It seemed
to take forever for her to come back on the line. "I just talked
to Bea, and she said if you can be here by nine, she'd be happy
to see you."

Tears of gratitude flooded my eyes. "I'll be there."

I followed the smell of burning sweetgrass down to Bea's office. She held out her arms.

"Before you tell me all about it, let's smudge." She brought the sweetgrass over to me, the three strands of the braid symbolizing a balance of mind, body and spirit. I was in desperate need of some balancing.

"There you are. That'll help. Now, cut to the chase and tell me: what's goin' on?"

"I saw Jessie this weekend."

My words hung heavy in the air.

"Okay, then." I knew Bea got how big this was for me. Jessie had crushed my trust in men—and in myself.

"We knew this day would come when you were strong enough to deal with it."

"I guess, Bea, but seeing him like that brought up so much for me."

"Well, my girl, this is a good chance for you. It's as if the Creator put him there this weekend so you could decide to truly let go and move on." She paused to allow me to sit with this. "So, shall we go through the story again and see if there's anything new to learn?"

I hesitated—I didn't want to revisit all that pain.

"Now don't go gettin' into analysis paralysis over this one. Let your heart decide." Bea looked at me affectionately, then got up from her chair to put the kettle on.

"Okay, let's do it. I'm just gonna talk." I took a deep breath. "It was Grand Entry on Saturday afternoon, and the drum group had begun singing the veterans, Elders and dancers into the arbour. Of course, out of respect, everyone stood up. It was then that I noticed him, way across the arbour. I saw his hat first, just as he removed it for the Honour song. I knew that hat, Bea. I knew that hat and the eagle feather attached to it. The irony of seeing him again, after all this time, on the drumbeat of an Honour song!" Tears streamed down my cheeks, leaving a salty trail. I paused for a few moments, the memory vivid. "The power of our connection was still strong, Bea. You might not believe this, because it seems too corny, but just after he removed his hat he turned and our eyes met—across the arbour."

Our gaze held, I told Bea. It was Bette who whispered to me, "What are you looking at, Tilly?" Her eyes must have followed where I was looking because I heard her catch her breath and then felt her warm hand on my arm. She said, "Tilly, look at me." I did. Then she asked, "You want to leave?"

I turned my eyes back to him again. I wanted to run out of there as fast as I could. But I knew that I'd be giving my power over to him, and on that long drive home from his community I'd promised myself I'd never do that again.

I said to Bette, "No. No, I want to stay."

"Okay, Tilly, you're one brave woman." She smiled at me and squeezed my arm.

As I finished telling my story to Bea, I found myself surprised at how brave I had been.

"So I have to ask," Bea said. "Did he ever come over?"

"Nope. He never did, and we never ran into each other. After a bit I looked over to where he'd been sitting, and he was gone."

Bea smiled at me. "You know what the Elders say, Tilly. There are no accidents. Everything happens for a reason." She handed me a cup of tea and settled herself comfortably back in her chair.

"Now we'll start from the beginning. Tell me again how you met this Jessie."

CHAPTER 31

Tears Are Medicine

BEA CALLED TO REMIND ME about the AA roundup the following Friday night. In my three years of sobriety, I'd never been to a roundup, one of the big gatherings that bring together people in AA from all over to listen to speakers and attend AA meetings. Nor had I ever been out with Bea in a public setting, away from the safety of her office nest.

We met at the front door of the arena, and she led us inside to register. I was surprised at how full the place was. Being there with Bea felt weird, but I trusted her, and I knew she must have some reason for inviting me to join her. As soon as we'd found seats, people started coming over to greet her. She stood to hug each of them, listening as if they were the only ones in the room. I was amazed at how present she was with everyone, and I thought back to an earlier homework assignment she'd given me.

"This week, you need to give a gift to everyone you spend time with. *Everyone*," she'd instructed.

"How is that possible, Bea?" I'd asked, confused.

"I want you to be fully present with each person you spend time with. Give them your full attention, look them in the eye and let them know you're listening. People just need to be seen and heard, Tilly. And you know what? It doesn't take much effort for us to offer them that. You know what it's like to feel someone is pretending to listen. Your homework is to genuinely see and listen to each person."

"Even the cashier at the grocery store?" I'd asked. "What if I'm in a hurry?"

"Everyone," Bea had said emphatically. "You never know who might have a story or teaching for you, or whose day you could brighten."

And now, in an arena full of five hundred alcoholics in recovery, I was witnessing Bea gift each person she spoke to with the magic of being fully present. It was extraordinary to see how each of them walked away a little taller.

"Ladies and gentlemen, please take your seats. We'll begin our roundup in five minutes."

My nervousness got the better of me, and I snuck out to use the washroom. I returned just in time to hear a woman at the podium announce: "Hello, my name is Sue, and I'm an alcoholic." All five hundred of us responded. "Hi, Sue." It gave me goosebumps.

Sue continued. "I have the honour of being your Mistress of Ceremonies for the evening." She laughed. "Being a mistress was part of my illness as an alcoholic, so being up here as the Mistress for five hundred other alcoholics, well, I find that quite funny." There was a great uproar of laughter, and everybody in the room seemed to relax a bit. Or maybe it was just me.

Sue went over the agenda for the evening and then introduced the next speaker. "Please put your hands together for Chuck." She opened her arms and welcomed a tall Native man to the podium.

Chuck started with the usual AA introduction, but there was nothing usual about his story. He told us he'd had his first sip of moonshine at the age of eight. "And I never looked back until I was twenty-eight, the first time I sobered up. That first taste of sobriety lasted for a couple of years and allowed me to see my daughters again. But my wife was in her right mind, and she wouldn't let me see *her* anymore. I was heartbroken and had no way to deal with it." His voice cracked, and he brought his hand up to wipe away tears.

I choked up myself. There was something about men crying that almost always affected me that way. Then I noticed Bea had tears streaming down her face and falling onto her white blouse. I felt like a child seeing a parent cry for the first time—vulnerable and helpless to make it better.

Chuck continued speaking. "Sometimes I'm surprised by how much pain I still feel at losing my family. I think I've got it all together, and then it's like I get sideswiped and the wind is knocked out of me. Somewhere I learned that it wasn't manly to cry. I've heard so many of our men say the same thing. But I've been teaching myself that it's okay to cry, that tears are medicine."

He paused for a moment to blow his nose and take a long drink of water.

"Over the years I've learned that both laughter and tears are medicine. As men, we've gotten unbalanced with both.

We use laughter to cover up our pain or to avoid deep connection. Sarcasm is part of that. I know I'm not gonna be too popular with some of you men for saying that, but it's what I've seen in our people."

AA had kept him alive and sober, Chuck said, but he'd needed deeper healing than the program or his sponsor could give him. "We didn't have all the counselling and treatment centres we do now, and since I was living in the city I didn't have access to the ceremonies, medicines or healers that could've helped me. So I only stayed sober for a couple years, and then I was back out there. I played hard. It still amazes me my liver functions after all those years."

For the rest of the hour, Chuck talked about his experience as a Native man. "It's about dads learning to be dads, uncles learning to be uncles and grandpas learning to be grandpas. I call it the Modern Day Warrior Ceremony. The learning, sharing and healing that happens at a ceremony never leaves you. It stays with you always. Some of our people believe the healing we do gets passed on to the following generations as well. So we aren't only healing ourselves, we're making sure our children don't experience the same pain. We need to support our men to find their way back to their rightful role as contributors to the wellness of their families, communities and Nations. Let's focus on breaking the unhealthy cycles and rebuilding healthy and traditional ones. That's what it's all about, folks." The audience broke into claps and cheers.

"Let me close by giving you a couple examples of things that have had an impact on my life and my career as an alcoholic." Men's traditional roles had been devalued and

undermined by Canadian legislation, he said: the imple-
mentation of the reserve system, the elected leadership that
was forced onto us instead of our hereditary systems, the loss
of hunting and fishing rights, disenfranchisement and the loss
of status, the introduction of welfare, Indian day schools and
residential schools.

"As a result of all this," he continued, "we lost our purpose,
our responsibility and our meaning as men. Loads of us are still
searching for that meaning." Chuck wiped his forehead with
the back of his hand. "I better wrap up here soon, or they're
going to escort me off the stage. Guess it's better than being
tossed out of a bar. Lord knows, I've been tossed out of
many a bar in my time." Again, laughter erupted. Many of us
listening to him could relate.

"Men, we've got a long journey ahead of us to be able to
walk honourably beside our women. We think we've done lots
of healing, but really, we're still just babies. Our children and
grandchildren, for some of us our great-grandchildren—they
need us to heal and find our meaning. Or maybe we need to
create it." He took a deep breath and seemed to be looking in
our direction—right at Bea and me. "And to the women out
there, thank you for all you've done to keep us alive. Thank
you for taking care of our families and for taking care of us
when we weren't strong enough to take care of ourselves.
You are powerful givers of life. I hope you are always treated
with respect and dignity. Thanks for listening and for helping
me stay sober for one more day. All my relations."

Along with the rest of the crowd, I jumped to my feet,
giving Chuck a standing ovation. I was still clapping when

I saw Bea pick up her purse and sling it over her shoulder. She leaned over to me and said, "I need fresh air, Tilly. Goin' outside for a bit. You're welcome to join me if you want." She turned and was gone, faster than I had ever seen her move.

I stopped at the concession on my way out to get a hot drink for both of us. When I found Bea, she was leaning against a tree with her eyes closed, rubbing a rock between her thumb and forefinger. I stood for a few moments relishing the fresh, cool air.

I was startled when Bea started to talk, her eyes still closed. "We were married once, Chuck and me. He's the father to my three oldest girls."

"Really, Bea? He was your husband?"

"Uh-huh." She opened her eyes and looked at me for a moment. "His story tells you a lot about what our marriage was like. He was a boy then, and still was when we divorced almost twenty years later. He's done lots of healing since then, as you heard tonight. But sometimes the healing comes too late. Too much damage has been done. Chuck and I started over more times than I care to remember. Each time ended with my hopes crushed. I finally decided enough was enough. But I'll always be thankful for him and the gifts he gave me: our three girls—and my own sobriety."

Bea sipped the coffee I'd brought her. She turned to face me, her shoulder and hip still resting on the tree.

"When our daughters were taken away because we were too busy drinking, it was a wake-up call for both of us. My life was empty without my girls. I felt like I had no reason to live. It would've been easy to drink myself to death. But whenever

I lifted a beer and got it close to my lips, I saw one of their faces." Her voice trailed off, and I strained to hear her. "I just couldn't take it anymore, Tilly. So I decided to do whatever that social worker lady said I had to, and more. It's taken me a long time to come to it, but I'm grateful to that social worker for taking our girls away. I know it sounds crazy, but I'm not sure if anything else could've made me sober up."

I stood taking this all in. This time I was the one letting the space of silence be okay. Bea pulled out a tissue, wiping her eyes and nose.

"So, together, Chuck and I got sober. We found our way to AA. We got our girls back after a year—but we never got that year back. We missed first days of school, baby teeth falling out and Christmas with our girls. It was hell, pure hell. Seeing Chuck up there tonight brought it all back. I wanted you to hear his message, maybe give you some insight into Jessie. But I didn't think I'd be out here havin' a boo-hoo."

I took a couple of steps towards Bea and hesitantly put my arms around her. It felt awkward but right to be the one giving support. She held on for a long time.

"Thanks, Tilly. I needed that." She lifted her glasses to wipe away the last of her tears. "I feel better now."

It was a good thing, since out of the corner of my eye I saw Chuck heading our way. She turned just as he reached us, as if she could sense his presence.

"Beautiful Bea." His voice was soft and warm. "I sure was hoping I'd see you here." He extended his arms for a hug. "May I?" he asked. She stepped forward into his open arms.

I headed for the arena, and just before I reached the door,

I heard someone calling me. "Tilly, over here." It was Mick, a social worker who referred youth to the suicide prevention program I ran. I didn't know him well, but he had always intrigued me. I waved hello, and he came over. "Hi. Hope I'm not invading your privacy," he said.

"No, not at all. I'm getting more and more comfortable with people knowing I'm in recovery."

"Me, too." He smiled. I hadn't noticed before how handsome he was. His hazel eyes held mine for a moment, and his cheeks flushed.

"That was quite the talk by Chuck, eh?" he said.

"Yes, it was." I glanced over at Bea and Chuck, who were now talking intently.

Mick's voice drew my attention back. "They're getting ready for the next speaker. Would you like to sit together?"

It was as if my mouth had a mind of its own. Before I could think of a response, I'd already said, "Sure." Mick held the door open, and I walked through.

CHAPTER 32

Decisions

MY FEELINGS WERE SO CHURNED UP after the roundup
that I called to make another urgent appointment with Bea.
Once again, she found room to fit me in. "So what's happening, Tilly?"

I tucked my legs up under me, getting comfortable in the
chair. "Ever since last Friday night, I keep replaying what
Chuck said. You know, about why our men are the way they
are, and, well, I guess I'm thinking more specifically about
why Jessie is the way he is."

Bea held up her hand, surprising me with the expression
on her face. "Before we go any farther with this, I need to tell
you about the fire. One of the teachings I had was about
bringing a problem or hurt to the fire. A person has the right
to bring that problem to the fire four times and have it listened
to by those sitting round the fire. In return, you must take
their guidance or direction and continue to move forward in
your healing. If you don't, you no longer have the right to
bring your problem to the fire or to seek guidance. Now, you

and me, we've talked about Jessie and moving on three times. I'm not being of service to you if I keep sitting here listening without challenging you to let go."

I kept my eyes trained on the carpet. I couldn't look at Bea just yet. Time seemed to stop as I decided what was next for me.

"You've been working hard, Tilly, and that's why I'm doing this. It's time to let go and to forgive. Forgiveness is one of the hardest things to do, but also so important in our healing."

I felt myself choke up. I didn't want to do either of those, let go or forgive, because then there would be no more excuses. I knew that not letting go of Jessie was keeping me stuck, but I was okay with that. I could blame him and not have to be accountable for my actions.

"This will be our last time to talk about him, Tilly, and about your relationship. I'm going to challenge you to be bigger than you think you can be." Bea looked at me over her glasses. "How ya doin' over there?"

I actually wasn't sure. My emotions were all jumbled up, and I was having a hard time focusing. "I'm scared, Bea, afraid to face the fact that all those dreams I had for us are never going to be reality."

"I hear a *but* in there, though," Bea said softly.

"But…" I swallowed hard. "I think I'm ready."

"Okay, here's what we're gonna do. I'll clear my schedule for the afternoon, and you and I will go down to the river. We'll sit so the river is flowing downstream from your heart, and you're going to tell me the whole Jessie story again from start to finish. The hurt in your heart, and all the tears you've been storing up, the river will take out to the ocean. Remember what Chuck said last week? Tears are medicine. We'll go get ourselves a strong dose of medicine today."

I didn't have time to argue. Bea stood up, put on her jacket and grabbed the Thermos off her desk. I followed her down the hall, knowing there was no turning back.

Suddenly I heard Grandma Tilly's voice. "It doesn't necessarily matter what the decision is, Tilly: just decide. Too many people think far too much for their own good. Make a decision and then begin actin' on it. Good things will start to flow your way. Trust in that."

I was finally ready to forgive and let Jessie go and allow good things to flow to me again.

CHAPTER 33

Mick

IN THE COUPLE OF YEARS SINCE MICK AND I had met up at the roundup, he and I had become good friends. We played together on a mixed slo-pitch team, went to ceremony together and shared dinner at least once a week. It was easy to be around him. I loved how he could make me laugh, often so hard my stomach ached. And I could talk to him about anything. We didn't always agree on how we saw situations or the world, but I always felt he respected my views— and me.

Mick was also of mixed ancestry, Cree and Scottish. He was the oldest of four children, the only boy. His parents, happily married after thirty-five years, still lived in Mick's childhood home. I found it easy to be around his family, and I spent many holidays hanging out with them.

It was at one of our weekly dinners that I realized my feelings for him had changed. I was preparing to move to Vancouver in a few weeks to start a new job. I'd known I would miss Mick, but it wasn't until I looked across the table at him that I realized how much. "You know, it's probably a good thing I'm moving," I said.

The noise in the restaurant seemed to diminish, and I could hear my heart pounding.

"What?" Mick asked, sounding slightly annoyed, as he looked up from his plate.

Our eyes connected and my heart lurched.

Mick put down his fork. "What do you mean, it's a good thing you're moving?" he said, a little more gently now.

We stared at each other for a few moments, each breath changing the course of our relationship.

"What are you really trying to say, Tilly?" Mick asked.

I wasn't sure.

Or was I?

I looked at him—his high cheekbones, black hair cut short and slightly spiked on the top, the dimple in his chin. He cocked his head to the side a bit as he looked back at me.

Mick had become my safe place to land, and I was only just waking up to that.

What if he didn't feel the same way? It was a risk, but what mattered most was that I was honest with him—and myself—about my feelings.

"I think I've fallen in love with you, Mick." My stomach flipped.

"You think?" His eyes narrowed. "Or you know?"

Before I could respond, he added, "Because *I* know." He held my gaze, and his voice softened. "I've loved you since the day I held the door for you at the roundup. I've been waiting until you were ready. I hoped the time would come, just didn't think it would take this long." He laughed, and I couldn't help but laugh, too.

He reached across the table, and I put my hand in his. It made me think about the last time I had held someone's hand like this. It was when Molly, Jessie's mom, and I sat at her kitchen table that fateful evening. I was a different person now. On my best days, I knew without a doubt that I was strong and courageous.

"I have to say, though, your timing sucks," Mick continued. We laughed again. He was right.

"Guess you'll just have to move to Vancouver yourself," I said. I was joking, but my stomach fluttered at my bold words.

CHAPTER 34

Billy's Braids

MY WORK WITH ABORIGINAL YOUTH had taught me the importance of strong, healthy families and communities, and my new job involved sharing what I knew through writing and giving presentations. The work was exciting and challenging, and it took me across the country. At one of the conferences I was invited to, I met Billy. He came to the front of the room right after my talk, waiting patiently while I spoke with another conference participant.

Billy towered over everyone else in the room, standing well over six feet. He wore a turquoise ribbon shirt that made his brown skin look radiant. Trendy jeans and polished dress shoes completed his outfit, and his shiny black hair was pulled back in a braid. He had high cheekbones, teardrop-shaped eyes and big full lips.

It was more than how distinguished this man looked, though, or how handsome he was—there was *something* about him. Before I could introduce myself, Billy reached out to hug me. He smelled good—not of some expensive cologne, but instead the soul-soothing smell of sweetgrass that lingers on your clothing after smudging. He felt like an old friend, or a big brother.

As we stepped back from our hug, Billy wiped each of his brown eyes with a thumb. "I'm sorry, but your presentation and stories, well, they..." He paused and looked towards the door for a moment. "I felt like you were telling my story. Especially when you talked about finding your own way back to your people, to the traditional ways."

I touched his forearm gently. "Here, let's sit down." I motioned for us to move to a table.

"Sorry, I didn't even introduce myself. My name's Billy, and it sure isn't like me to come and talk to you like this. I was just packing up my briefcase back there, and then next thing I knew, here I was." He shook his head. "It was as if someone, or something, pushed me up here."

I knew the force he spoke of, the one that propels us forward when we might not otherwise have the courage. I think of it as our Ancestors supporting us to move towards what's best for us at a certain point in time.

"All of this, being at a healing conference, crying in public, talking to people about myself—it's all new for me," Billy continued. "When you talked about all the Aboriginal kids who were taken away from their homes and their parents in the 1960s and put in non-Native foster homes, that was me. I've never heard that term before, Sixties Scoop. But that's what I am...I'm a Sixties Scoop kid." He pulled his black leather wallet from his back pocket and opened the photo holder. "Let me show you my girls."

Billy beamed as he went through the photos one by one. There were pictures of his daughters when they were babies, at their christenings and at their Aboriginal Head Start graduations.

"Hmm, haven't looked at this photo for a long time," he said, pulling out an old Polaroid. It was worn and tattered, with the colours badly faded.

"My birth mom gave me this the day we were reunited. It's the only photo I have of my birth family. A couple months after this was taken, all of us kids were put in foster care or sent to residential school."

Billy stayed quiet for a moment, his finger resting on the photo. "That little guy there, smiling so wide, that's me." He shook his head. "The next picture I have of me was taken at the first foster home I went to. The lady there cut off my braids—snipped them off with two squeezes of her scissors and threw them in the garbage. Can you believe that?"

Unfortunately, I could. Billy's experience was like that of so many others who had survived the Sixties Scoop, I'd learned. At the time, most foster families thought the best thing they could do for the Indian children in their care was to make them look and act as white as possible. Instead, these children lost their pride, their languages and their culture. They lost the sense of knowing who they were.

I remembered Bea's teaching about sitting with someone quietly, how important it can be to allow healing to unfold. Billy looked up from the photo after a few moments. "I didn't know until my daughter was in Head Start that in our teachings a braid is real important, and that wearing two of

168

them means both parents are living. So when that lady cut my braids off, it was like she cut off my connection to my family and to who I was. Every day since, though I didn't realize it until a few years ago, I've been trying to reconnect with my Creeness." He smiled. "I don't know if that's even a word, Creeness, but it fits."

Billy had never been able to really connect with his birth mom, he told me. "We're really different from each other, and we haven't been able to find a way to bridge those differences and have a relationship." His voice softened. "It's sort of been like losing her twice. And my birth dad, he passed over to the other side a few months before I was reunited with everyone. All those times I thought about looking for them but wasn't ready, it never occurred to me that they wouldn't both be alive."

He folded the Polaroid photo in half and tucked it back into his wallet. "I'm not sure if you're free, but I was going to skip the next workshop and go for coffee. There's a Tim Hortons across the street calling my name."

Once we were settled in with our coffee, I told Billy about my mom. She'd finally decided the time was right to search for her birth family, but she'd been trying to find them now for more than five years. I understood Billy's longing for connection.

"My wife, she's the one who really opened me up to being Native," he said. "She's Métis and grew up knowing her culture and speaking Michif. Now she's teaching our girls the language. She's so rich in her culture, knowing who she is and where she comes from. I often feel bankrupt, not knowing my culture in the same way. Instead, my girls are teaching me. I heard an Elder say once that whichever parent has the most to learn about the opposite sex, that's what determines the gender their child will be. Guess since I have three girls and no boys, I've got a lot to learn about women, eh?" He chuckled. "I'm always going to events at the Friendship Centre and Head Start, as well as the gatherings and ceremonies in my community. It's like I can't get enough. And each time I feel like a little bit more of me has woken up from a deep sleep."

Billy had been lucky in one way, he told me over a second cup of coffee. He and his sister Kathy were adopted by the same family, and their adoptive mom had always made it clear to them that, when they were ready, she would tell them everything she knew about their birth family and help their search in whatever way she could. It was the birth of his first daughter that was the catalyst for Billy to begin looking.

"I went to my mom when my oldest girl was a couple weeks old and told her I was ready. She said to me, 'Well, then, I'm going to put the coffee on and cut us a piece of saskatoon pie. You go upstairs and get your box.' That box was tucked under the bed in my old room. It held my first drawings, all my report cards, my school photos, my grad photo from business school and my first ball glove. What I didn't realize was that my adoptive mom had tucked my adoption information in there, too."

It was eight years since he had opened that envelope, he told me, and he was a different man because of it. "Me and my seven brothers and sisters were taken away from our parents in 1969. I was the baby, only five years old, and Kathy was almost seven. I don't know why we got put into foster care; our older siblings were sent to residential schools."

When Billy had finally tracked down his birth mom and his siblings, he said, he saw different parts of himself in each of them. He had the same teardrop-shaped eyes as his mom. All three brothers were over six feet tall and had the same strong, sinewy build. With his sisters he shared distinctive cheekbones and a few freckles. "It happened really fast, and it was exciting and frightening at the same time. I was ready for it. Kathy, on the other hand, she wasn't interested in meeting our family. I think she remembers more than I do from our life before we were taken away. She's come around a bit, but she's still very protective of her heart."

Billy drained his cup. "I know we have to get back to the conference, but do you want to hear something wild, Tilly? My oldest brother and I realized that we'd gone to the University of Saskatchewan at the same time, even had a class together. How's that for crazy?"

As we stood to go, I thought again about my mom's search. Billy's story had touched me deeply. What would my mom discover when she finally met her own birth family?

CHAPTER 35 ·

Family

I WASN'T SURE WHEN I'D FALLEN ASLEEP. It had been all I could do to roll my sweatshirt into a makeshift pillow, and then I was out. I was exhausted, the kind of tired where every bone in your body aches and you can't keep your eyes open. My work that week, in an isolated First Nation, had been gratifying, humbling and intense. Since that first summer, when Mabel had asked me to work with her, I'd heard many heart-wrenching stories in communities all across Canada. I was always left in awe at the strength of the human spirit and our resilience as Aboriginal people.

The thump as the ferry docked at its next stop stirred me from my deep sleep. But the sun shining through the window was almost blinding, and it provided me with a good excuse to close my eyes again. I was just drifting off when a man's voice woke me. I opened my eyes to check things out.

"Um, excuse me, miss, the ferry is pretty full, so I'm wondering if I can have this seat." He motioned to the seat that I had my legs curled up on.

"Oh, I'm sorry." I swung my legs down to the floor.

"Not to worry," the man said as he slid his suitcase under the seat in front of him. He placed a small cooler and Thermos by his feet. He hitched his pants up towards his waist as he sat down.

"There're usually lots of empty seats on this ferry, now that the road has been built. But me, I like the tranquility of being out on the ocean." He extended his hand. "Pardon my rudeness. My name is Saul."

I shook his hand. "Nice to meet you, Saul. My name's Tilly."

"Pleasure's all mine."

I smiled. Normally I'd find some excuse to remove myself from further conversation, but there was something about this Aboriginal man that drew me to him. He had the face of a little boy and a dimple in his chin. His hair was black, with a few grey wisps around his temples, and it was combed back and held in place with a copious amount of Brylcreem. His red cowboy shirt was unbuttoned at the neck, exposing a gold cross on a chain, and he had a cigarette pack in his chest pocket. Saul's sleeves were rolled up to just below his elbows, revealing hairless arms and a variety of tattoos. They looked as if they'd been done by a friend or while Saul was in jail or serving in the Navy. His black cowboy boots were freshly polished.

"Where you from, Tilly?" he asked. I knew what he meant. Not where did I live, but something much deeper: what community was I from, what Nation was I from, who were my people.

"Long version or short version?" I said, fully awake now and revitalized from my nap.

"Now I'm intrigued. Let's go with the long version." He smiled at me and raised his eyebrows. His eyes danced.

"Well, where do I begin?" I shifted in my seat to face him. "I'm mixed heritage."

"Seems we're all mixed heritage these days. But go on, tell me more about your family."

"On my mom's side, I'm Cree from Saskatchewan. I don't know which community I'm from because she was removed from her parents at birth and placed in an orphanage. My dad's family is of Lakota ancestry. They moved to Canada in the 1930s, when my Grandma Tilly was little."

"Did your mom grow up in the orphanage?" Saul asked.

"No, she was only there until she was three. A friend of my grandma and grandpa's worked at the orphanage and knew my grandparents were considering adoption, so she told them about this little girl with dark curly hair she felt they just had to meet. They took a trip down to the orphanage, not anticipating coming home with this little girl, but they did. They came home with my mom."

"Did your grandparents already have kids?"

"Yeah, they had my aunt, who was about five then, but they both came from large farming families and they wanted to have a large family themselves."

"Were they Indian?"

"No, English and German. My mom was raised in a primarily German community, and she was the only Indian there." Mom's story was spilling out as if I couldn't stop myself. And it felt good. "She told me that one of the best days of her life was the day a Chinese family moved to town and opened a restaurant. She was so happy to no longer be the only non-white person in her town." I turned to look out the window for a moment. The landscape of the wild west coast passed slowly before my eyes: rocks shaped by tides for generations, cedar trees with boughs so thick you couldn't see past the edge of the forest. I wondered what lived in there, beyond what we knew.

I turned back to him. "You know, Saul, I have no idea why I'm telling you all this."

He smiled. "Yeah, everyone tells me I should have been a counsellor instead of an accountant. I learned to listen from being with my grandpa out on his fishing boat or off hunting. There was no option but to listen. Spending my teen years in an Indian hospital surrounded by women, I'm sure that helped, too." He chuckled.

"An Indian hospital?"

"Yep. I had tuberculosis," he responded. "And that story requires a cup of coffee." He leaned forward and picked up his Thermos. "I have another mug in my cooler. Would you like a cup? It's already doctored up with cream and sugar. Well, not really cream, evaporated milk. Even better."

"Sure, I'd love a coffee."

He poured out a cup and handed it to me, then poured one for himself. "I have salmon sandwiches, too, if you're hungry. Caught and canned it myself."

"No, thanks."

He pulled a sandwich from the cooler and sat back to

unwrap it. "I have to back up a few years before the Indian hospital, though, or the story won't make any sense." The delicious smell of salmon wafted between us as he took a bite. "Late summer days like this always remind me of the first time I rode this ferry. My life changed that day. I know that sounds dramatic, but it's true. When I think of my life, I always divide it into two categories: Before Residential School and After Residential School. That first ferry ride divides things." He took another bite of his sandwich, chewed for a bit and had a sip of his coffee. I could tell this story was not one to be rushed. I was content to sip my coffee and wait.

"See that space there, between those small islands?" Saul pointed out the window. "That's where my grandpa's boat was the morning the five of us left. He was out on the bow, and he waved as we passed. That was the last time I saw him alive, and I can still picture him standing there. What my brothers and sisters and I didn't know when we got on the ferry, and what our parents didn't know when they said goodbye to us, was that we would all be sent to different schools. That morning we stood waiting for the ferry was the last time my whole family would ever be together." His eyes filled with tears. "That was forty-six years ago, Tilly. Not a day goes by that I don't wonder how our lives would have been different if we hadn't gotten on that ferry. But I can't think of it for long—makes me crazy with rage. And that don't do anyone any good."

His honesty moved me, and my eyes stung. Saul cleared his throat.

"Sure, I see my brothers and sisters every now and then. My brother and I are the only ones who've moved back home to the reserve. The rest live in the city. I'm not sure what they'd do if they came back home. I'm not even sure they'd call this home anymore. They've created their own sense of community there in the city, and it works for them." He crossed his legs, folding the wax paper that had held his sandwich into small squares. "People are just starting to talk about those schools and all the horrible things that happened there."

In his language, he told me, the word for "child" had many meanings. One of them was "the purpose for my living." "You can imagine what happens to a community when their entire purpose for living is taken away. I guess in some ways I was lucky. I didn't go to residential school until I was ten, so I had a lot of time with my grandpa and my dad. They taught me our ways, our ceremonies, our songs, how to navigate and fish these waters." He nodded towards the window. "My mom, well, there aren't really any words in English to describe her. She was the most beautiful woman. And smart, holy, was she smart! But she was never the same after we were sent to school. It was like the happiness in her heart died, though she kept on living."

Saul reached into his cooler and pulled out a plastic container. He flipped the lid and handed the container to me. "You gotta have one. My wife's secret recipe."

I helped myself to a cookie and took a bite. "Mmmm."

"I know, eh? Now, where was I? Oh yeah, like I could forget. Family. I think the government set up those schools because

177

they were scared of us and our family structures—how powerful we were. And how powerful we still are."

Saul's story was making me think more about my mom's. She was still looking for her birth family. A social worker in Regina supposedly had the status number of my mom's birth father on file, as well as the name of the band he was registered with, but my mom had met roadblock after roadblock in trying to get that information. I admired many things about my mom, and one of them was her tenacity. I knew that one day she would find her birth parents. Until then, all I could do was support her. At the Kamloops Pow Wow a few weeks before, she'd turned to me and said, "You know, Tilly, I could be sitting beside my cousin here, or maybe even my sister." Her comment had run through my mind many times since then. I felt helpless to ease her turmoil, her sense of not knowing where she belonged.

It was as if Saul was reading my mind. "There are so many of us trying to find our way back to our families now. Culture and ceremony are what's kept me alive—even when I wasn't sure I wanted to be alive. Of course, I guess lots of people would consider me lucky for having spent only three years at that school. They were long years, though. I came home for Christmas the first year, but after that the school said it cost too much money to get me home and back again."

"What happened after those three years?" I asked.

He rubbed his chin with his hand. "I need a smoke before I go into that part of the story. You want to come up on deck with me and get some fresh air? You can see so much more from up there."

As he puffed on his cigarette, Saul explained that he had contracted tuberculosis near the end of his third year at school and had been sent to the Coqualeetza Indian Turberculosis Hospital in Sardis. It was horribly lonely lying in a hospital bed day after day. "Lots of people ask me if I got bored," he said. "Sure, at times I did, but it wasn't the boredom that haunted me. It was how alone I was, and how much I missed my family."

He would pass the time, he told me, by counting the tiles in the panelling on the ceiling or figuring out how many beds the hospital had. One nurse took a liking to him, and she'd bring in her son's math and calculus textbooks. Saul devoured them. As he got better, and was able to get up and about, the nurse convinced him to study for the grade twelve exams. When he was eighteen, Saul graduated from high school without having ever attended a day.

"That nurse, Ruth, she saw my gift with numbers. She's the reason I'm an accountant today. Outside of my family, she was the first person who ever believed in me, who challenged and supported me. My wife and I, we named our oldest daughter after her."

Before I knew it, it was time for us to say goodbye. The ferry ride had taken just three hours, but I felt like I'd known Saul for a lifetime.

"My daughter's picking me up, and we're heading over to a gathering at the Friendship Centre. Want to join us?"

"I'd love to, but I have to get to the airport to catch my flight home to Vancouver."

"Well, then, let's just say 'see ya.' There's no such word as goodbye in my language. Way too final." He smiled. "I don't usually talk about all that stuff, Tilly. It's in the past, and that's usually where I like it to stay. But today, it felt good to talk. Well, maybe *good* isn't the right word. It was healing." He stepped forward and hugged me. "You take good care of yourself, and help your mom. One day she'll find her family. I really believe that."

The honk of a car horn startled both of us.

"Well, there's my ride. Look forward to our paths crossin' again one day." With a wave of his hand, Saul picked up his cooler and his suitcase and headed off.

CHAPTER 36

Multiple Blessings

MICK HADN'T MOVED TO VANCOUVER right away. We took turns travelling to see each other at first. It wasn't the easiest arrangement, but we managed. Each time I travelled home to see him and my family, I also saw Bea. My relationship with Mick was completely different from what I'd had with Jessie, but I needed to learn how to trust again and how to be in a healthy relationship. Bea helped me with that.

Then Mick was accepted to do his master's degree at the University of British Columbia. That August we moved into our first place together. A year later we were married in the backyard of his parents' house, standing under his childhood tree fort to make our vows. It was a small gathering of witnesses—our families, Bette, a few of Mick's friends, Mabel and Bea—and it was, without question, one of the most beautiful days of my life.

Things were sometimes challenging in our relationship, but we worked hard at communicating, and our long friendship gave us a solid base. Four years into our marriage, Mick had finished school and was working full-time. I continued doing workshops across Canada. I came home from one work trip with what I thought was a nasty stomach flu. After I'd been bedridden for days, exhausted and not able to keep anything down, Mick demanded I see our doctor, who sent me for blood tests.

A couple of days later, the phone rang.

"Tilly, this is Dr. Peterson's office. We've received your blood test results, and the doctor would like to see you. We have an opening tomorrow at noon, would that work?"

Mick and I arrived early the next day, sitting nervously in the waiting room. Finally we were shown to an examining room. Dr. Peterson followed us in.

"I have what I think will be good news for the two of you," she said. "One of the blood tests I ordered was a pregnancy test, and it came back positive."

I felt Mick's hand cover mine. Even before I looked at him, I knew his smile was as wide as mine.

Dr. Peterson grinned. "Hop up here on the examining table, Tilly, so we can listen to the baby's heartbeat."

Once I'd lain back and lifted my shirt over my stomach, Dr. Peterson slid a small monitor around on my belly until we heard *boom-boom, boom-boom*.

"There it is," she said. "Your baby's heartbeat. There's something else I want to check out, too." She continued to move the monitor across my tummy until we heard it again: *boom-boom, boom-boom*.

"That's what I thought," she said. "You two are having twins."

"Twins?" Mick and I said in unison.

"Yes, twins." She looked down at her clipboard, then back up at us, smiling broadly. "Congratulations. You'll make wonderful parents."

Our daughter, Piper, and our son, Grayson, were born just after midnight on an October full moon. Mick took a parental leave, and we spent the first year planting our family roots deep into the earth. Although I wasn't prepared for the exhaustion or the sleep deprivation, the joy I felt in being a mom outweighed the challenges. Mick was a natural father, and I adored his tenderness and his affection for our babies. After the first three months, I started work again, focusing mainly on my writing. I'd squeeze in the time at my desk late at night or while the twins napped. It was quite an adjustment when Mick went back to work, too, but over time we established a good routine.

One day when the twins were almost three, I took advantage of their afternoon nap to get some housework done. I was washing the dishes when I heard the faint notes of the Women's Warrior song. I'd learned it from Mabel during the summer we spent together, and now, in my sleep-deprived state, I thought at first it was me singing; after all, no one else in our house knew the song that was softly filling the rooms. However, I soon realized that it wasn't me: it was the voice of a child. I followed the melodic voice down the hall towards the twins' room. As I got closer, I saw that it was Piper singing. I stood in the doorway, watching and listening. She was lying on her back, nestled under her comforter with her hands in the air. She was using the back of her right hand as a drumstick against the palm of her left one. The beat was perfect, like that of a heart. A thrill ran through my body. How did my daughter know this song? I had sung it almost daily while I was pregnant with the twins, and I'd sung it to them many, many times since then. But it was still a shock to hear it coming so perfectly from a toddler.

I closed my eyes. Piper's voice and the drumbeat of her little hands eased me into a peaceful state, erasing the stresses of my day. My daughter and I were connecting beyond our physical selves, beyond just the two of us. It felt as if the air itself danced around and within us. Mabel's words from that long-ago summer came back to me. "This is a song of great strength and beauty. Women have incredible power because we are the givers of life. Being warriors doesn't mean we have to fight or force our beliefs or ideas on others in an aggressive way. This song talks about the importance of speaking our truth, of living an honest and respectful life and honouring the beauty within each one of us."

Our children remember, Mabel had taught me.

The song my daughter was singing had been chanted for generations upon generations, and it would continue to be sung by generations to come.

CHAPTER 37

Courage

ONCE THE TWINS STARTED SCHOOL, I was able to travel for work more often. In May 2008, I attended a meeting in Ottawa to discuss programming for Aboriginal children and their families. At the time, there was a lot of talk in Indian country about the residential school apology that would soon be offered by Prime Minister Stephen Harper. People at the meeting had mixed emotions and different opinions about the apology. But when a non-Aboriginal woman made a comment about residential schools being far in the past, one of our colleagues spoke up to shatter that myth.

"I was in the final grad class of White Calf Collegiate. It was one of the last residential schools to close in Canada. That was 1996." She paused for a moment. "Only twelve years ago. The abuses that happened at the schools in the early years, they were still happening at my school, to both the girls and the boys."

A hush fell over the meeting. This young woman had had the courage to speak the unspoken, and no one knew quite how to respond.

It was an Elder, Sophie, who broke the silence. "I learned this saying once: What you live with, you learn; what you learn, you practise; and what you practise, you become— until you learn a new way."

I knew that saying. I'd heard it when I was in treatment fifteen years before.

Sophie continued. "Those schools, they took our traditional teachings away and replaced them with physical abuse, sexual abuse, hunger and loneliness. But it's the brave ones..." Looking directly at the woman who had shared her story, Sophie nodded her head and raised her eyebrows. "It's the brave ones like this young woman who will lead us and our families out of the darkness."

The room stayed quiet. Most of us were far too familiar with that darkness, both in our own lives and in the lives of the families we served.

Sophie sat forward in her chair and directed her gaze around the room, looking in turn at each of us. "It's time for us to learn new ways, so that our children and their children— the next seven generations—are free from experiencing those things that are too painful for us to even talk about."

She swiped her hand through the air, just as I had seen Grandma Tilly and Bea do when enough was enough.

"So, let's get on with this meeting. This is the work that will heal our families and ensure that our future generations don't have a childhood they have to recover from."

CHAPTER 38

Bay Street Dan

SIX MONTHS LATER, after three days of workshops in Toronto, I was exhausted and missing my family. When I boarded my flight back to Vancouver, I was relieved to discover that I had three seats to myself: a little piece of heaven. I got cozy in the window seat, put in my earplugs, closed my eyes and settled in for what I hoped would be a long nap. Just as I was floating between wakefulness and dream time, the scent of Aqua Velva cologne and cigarettes flooded my nostrils.

My eyelids were too heavy to open at first. But the scent of Aqua Velva transported me back in time. I was a young girl again, standing in the bathroom doorway watching my dad shave. As he balanced a cigarette between his lips, he updated me on the hockey game from the night before, then asked me what I was up to for the day.

I giggled. "Dad, I'm going to school. What do you think I'm up to?"

"About four feet." He gave me a wink.

After he'd finished shaving, he splashed Aqua Velva on his chin and cheeks.

"You know, my girl, one of these nights when your mom is out, you can stay up and watch the whole game with me." He smiled at me in the mirror, knowing how happy that would make me. I played road hockey with the boys whenever I could, always wearing my Montreal Canadiens number ten jersey in honour of my favourite player, Guy Lafleur.

My adult self drifted off to sleep, full of contentment at such a fond memory.

I awoke to turbulence and the beep of the seat-belt sign. I gave my eyes a rub, then looked over at my seatmate. He was resting comfortably, eyes closed, arms crossed, with one foot stuck out in the aisle. His tie was crooked and didn't really match his shirt. His suit jacket was a different colour again. His dark hair, grey strands woven throughout, hung down over his ears. His nose was pinkish and big, too big for his face. But he was attractive in a fatherly sort of way.

"Do you like what you see?"

I jumped at being caught.

"Don't you know you should let a sleeping man rest in peace?"

"Sorry," I mumbled.

Finally, he opened his eyes and grinned. "That's okay, don't be worryin' about it. I'm used to sleeping with one eye open. But you, you were out cold. You missed out on the free snacks. I kept the lunch for you." He pointed to the tray on the seat between us. "Just in case you woke up hungry."

"Thank you, sir."

188

He laughed. "Wow. Your parents taught you good manners. But please, my name is Dan." He offered me his hand. As I shook it, a warmth flooded my body.

"Nice to meet you. I'm Tilly."

"Tilly: now there's an old Indian name. Where you from, there, Miss Tilly?"

"I live in Vancouver, but my mom is Cree and Scottish from Saskatchewan, and my Grandma Tilly, my dad's mom, she was Lakota." I paused. There was something familiar about this man, but I couldn't put my finger on it. "How did you know I was Aboriginal?"

"Oh, that's easy. It's in your eyes. And our people can tell when they're with family. I'm Cree, too, from Saddle Lake. But I haven't been home for a very long time." He shifted in his seat to face me. "What community you from?"

The dreaded question. The sadness of not knowing exactly which community my mom was from was sometimes too much to bear, let alone talk about. But Dan sensed that quickly.

"It's okay. Lots of our people don't know which community they're from. So much has happened to us over the years that many of us are lost. Doesn't mean we don't know who we are inside, though sometimes knowing where we come from can help with that."

I nodded. "My mom and I have been looking for her family for years now, but it seems like every time we get close, the door slams in our faces. I feel like there are some missing pieces to the puzzle of who I am, and I get scared sometimes that I'll never find them. My mom gets discouraged, too.

When we're at a Pow Wow or a ceremony she often says to me, 'I wonder if I have relatives here. Do you see anyone who looks like me?'"

Tears welled up inside me, and I turned to look out the window. Dan gave me plenty of time before he responded.

"I been away from my own family and community for a real long time." He sighed. "I only been home to Saddle Lake once in the last fifty-four years, and that was when my Kokum died. You know what Kokum means, eh?"

I nodded. "Grandma."

"Well, she passed over to the spirit world when I was eighteen. She had written me a letter in Cree every week after I was taken away to residential school. I lived for those letters—they were my only connection to my home. Even though my Kokum could write in English, too, she wrote to me in syllabics. She wanted me to remember my language. Those schools didn't allow us to be speakin' Indian. They were trying to get as much Indian out of us as they could. Didn't work for me, though." He grinned. "I'm still Indian and always will be."

Having heard many stories of the residential schools, I wasn't sure what was respectful to ask him and what wasn't. So I proceeded cautiously. "How old were you when you were sent away to school?"

"I was five." He paused for a moment, gathering his thoughts. "I know some people think I should be grateful because I got a good education at that school. I graduated and could have gone on to college if I'd wanted. But gratitude isn't usually what I feel." His eyes grew darker, and he shuddered.

When he spoke again, it was about his family. "You might think I look too young to have a great-granddaughter." He smiled. "But that's why I'm going to Vancouver. I'm going to meet my great-granddaughter. My oldest girl's boy just had a baby girl. Well, he didn't have the baby, his girlfriend did."

I laughed.

"This is my chance, Tilly. My Kokum always said that the Creator gives us three chances to make a difference in this world, with our children, our grandchildren and our great-grandchildren. This new baby girl who's been sent to us, she's my third chance. My final chance. I don't wanna blow it."

Dan crossed his legs and rubbed his hand over his jaw a couple of times. When he started to speak again, his voice cracked. "I tried with my children. I really did. But it was a bad time for me. I couldn't keep a job. It seemed like at every job I got there was a guy who reminded me of that priest at residential school. And I didn't want to be reminded of him or what he had done to me. So I wouldn't go back to the job. Usually I'd get real drunk instead and not go home for days, sometimes weeks. In the end, my wife kicked me out. She said she felt like she was taking care of six kids when she had only given birth to five. She was right, you know. I was a big kid with too much pain in his heart to even begin to be a good husband. And a good dad...well, what they taught me at school about love was not what I wanted to teach my own children."

Melancholy swirled between us, each of us immersed in our own thoughts. Dan rested his head back against the seat, closing his eyes.

"Ain't we been through this once already, Tilly? Me catching you lookin' at me while I'm restin' my eyes?"

After a second, he turned his head to look at me, then started to laugh.

It felt good to laugh along with him.

"What's her name, your great-granddaughter?"

"They named her Grace. It was my Kokum's name."

I smiled. "I have a feeling you're going to have an amazing trip, Dan."

"That's another thing," he said. "It's nice to be called just plain Dan. I been known for so long as Bay Street Dan."

"Bay Street Dan?"

"Yep, because Bay Street in Toronto was my home. I lived on that street for over thirty years, up until my daughter came to find me. I was a mess. She got me into treatment and then a recovery home. I been sober now for eleven months and six days." He looked at his pocket watch. "And fifteen hours."

I understood what it felt like to know exactly when you'd had your last drink. "Wow, good for you. That's really something to be proud of."

"Thanks." For the first time since we'd started talking, Dan looked me right in the eye as he smiled.

Shivers went down my spine.

I knew that smile.

I'd seen it in my dreams many times. I'd called it to mind whenever I needed hope or courage. And the words that went with that smile had echoed in my head all these years. "Never question who you are or who your people are. It's in your eyes. I know it's in your heart."

My skin was covered in goosebumps.

"Dan," I said, "I think we might have met before. Well, more like briefly crossed paths. I wondered afterwards if you were even real, or if I was having some kind of vision. But just now, when you smiled at me, well…" I didn't have words to describe what was going on inside me.

He nodded. "I thought when I saw you you were the girl from the pub that day. You know, I hardly ever talk to people out on the street, especially not pretty young girls. That can get a guy like me into a lot of trouble." He smiled at me again.

That smile!

"But that day, it was like somebody pushed me over to you and told me what to say. I'd never had that experience before. And now here you are again. But you look different all these years later."

"Older, you mean?" I laughed.

"No, not that. It's like you grew up. You look now as if you have the pride of your Ancestors in your heart. Not the fear and confusion I saw in your eyes that day."

A voice came over the intercom, interrupting our conversation. "Ladies and gentlemen, we have begun our descent into Vancouver. Please ensure that your seat belts are securely fastened and your tray tables are in the secure, upright and locked position."

Dan ran his hand through his hair and adjusted his tie. "I guess we're almost there, Tilly. I can hardly believe I'm going to meet little Grace and see my family again. I've got a lot of catchin' up to do. It's scary, though. Still got a lot of demons in my closet."

"An amazing counsellor gave me some good advice one time," I said. "She told me never to get too hungry, angry, lonely or tired. HALT for short."

"I'll keep it in mind. And now, I'm gonna close my eyes for a moment and say a few prayers."

When we got to the baggage carousel, Dan's family was waiting. They had balloons and were holding up a sign: "Welcome home, Dad, Grandpa and Great-Grandpa." Soon everybody was crying and hugging him.

I had to look away for a moment, because witnessing the intimate homecoming was so moving. When I looked back, little Grace was being placed in Dan's arms. He held her to his chest like she was the most precious thing in the world.

CHAPTER 39

A Story to Tell

WE ALL GET MESSAGES, even if they don't come at the most convenient time. I was sound asleep in bed when I felt a tug on my foot. I thought it was one of the twins wanting to crawl into bed with us because of a bad dream. In my slumberous state, I mumbled, "Come on in, my love." I threw the covers back a bit to make room. But nobody crawled in.

I felt the tug again.

"Come on, my love," I said. "Crawl in here and stop playing games."

Again, nothing happened.

When I sat up, nobody was there. I got up to check on Piper and Grayson, but they were sleeping peacefully in their rooms.

Despite the coziness of our down-filled duvet and the warmth of Mick's body calling me back, I was wide awake by now. I knew trying to sleep would be futile.

I went to the living room, got my bundle out and started my morning routine of smudging and giving thanks. I had so much to be grateful for. I'd celebrated twenty years of sobriety and was immensely proud of that accomplishment. We had two healthy children who'd never seen me drink, and Mick and I had now been married for eleven years.

As I was reflecting on the many things I had to offer thanksgiving for, I remembered something Bea had told me. Sometimes she would get visits from the Ancestors, she said. They would come to her when she needed guidance or direction, and they always brought her a message.

Her voice echoed in my head. "It isn't necessarily the message I want to hear. But you know, when I listen, really listen, the message is always exactly what I *need* to hear."

The mysterious pulling on my toe signalled a visit from my Ancestors, I realized then. And they had a message for me. "Get up and write, Tilly. We have a story for you to tell."

GLOSSARY

The definitions that follow are not meant to be academic ones. Instead, they are based on the teachings I've received over the years and on my own knowledge and understanding.

Aboriginal is a term that's appropriate when referring to First Nations (Indian), Inuit and Métis peoples.

Aboriginal Head Start is a preschool for Aboriginal children focusing on Aboriginal culture and language, school readiness, health promotion, nutrition, social support and parental involvement.

All my relations is an expression used to honour the Aboriginal belief that family includes Ancestors, the generations to come, animals and plants. We are all interconnected.

An *altar* is a sacred space where ceremonies can be performed and where a bundle of sacred items is kept.

Ancestors are those in your family lineage who have passed on and watch over you, guide you and protect you.

An *arbour* is where ceremonies like the Pow Wow are held, always in a circle. It is considered sacred ground where no alcohol or drugs are to enter.

A *band* is typically, but not always, composed of a single Aboriginal community in Canada. Many bands, especially in British Columbia, govern more than one reserve. Most bands prefer to be referred to as First Nations.

The *band council* oversees the social, educational and economic development of the band's members. The chief and councillors are elected to a set term.

A **Big House** is a gathering and ceremonial place.

A **bundle** is a collection of items that have been given to you, have special meaning and contribute to your spiritual wellness. The bundle helps you in your development and can be used in ceremonies.

Circle time, also known as a healing circle, facilitates a better understanding of yourself, others and the issues at hand. In a circle, you must speak truthfully from the heart, be brief and listen attentively to others. There is no cross talk or interference when someone else is speaking.

The **Cree** Nation is one of the largest First Nations in Canada. There are Cree communities in B.C., Alberta, Saskatchewan, Manitoba, Quebec and the Northwest Territories.

Cree syllabics are symbols used to write Cree and some other Aboriginal languages.

Culture encompasses the traditions, history, values, beliefs and languages that make up your heritage. It helps you to understand your world and how you fit within it.

A **drum group** is a group of people who have dedicated time to learning and practising the traditional songs and who share these songs at cultural gatherings like Pow Wows.

Drums represent the heartbeat of each Nation and are considered sacred.

An **eagle feather** is often given as a sign of growth, change or rite of passage. When you are holding it, you must speak the truth from your heart and use kind, respectful words.

People become **Elders** in a variety of ways: through age, knowledge, wisdom, spiritual commitment and the respect of their people. Elders hold a special place in Aboriginal communities and are treated with respect and dignity.

First Nations is a term commonly used to describe the various societies of North American Indigenous peoples living in what is now Canada. It does not apply to people of Inuit or Métis ancestry.

A *food offering* is a plate of food prepared from a meal or feast. Tobacco is added to the offering, which is prayed over and then placed outside under a tree, symbolically feeding the Ancestors and future generations.

Friendship Centres provide culturally appropriate services and programs for Aboriginal people in urban settings. They usually combine traditional and modern practices, creating an environment in which people are comfortable to learn and grow.

The *Grand Entry* is the first ceremony of a Pow Wow and is used to bring in the chiefs and other dignitaries, Elders and dancers.

The *Great Spirit* is believed to have power over all things, including animals, trees, stones and clouds.

Haudenosaunee means the "People of the Longhouse." These people are also known as the Iroquois and include the Cayuga, Mohawk, Oneida, Onondaga, Seneca and Tuscarora Nations.

Honour songs are requested to honour individuals at a Pow Wow or ceremony. Spectators should always stand and remove their caps and hats for an Honour song.

Indian is a term with many usages. Historically, and still today, it refers to Canadians of First Nations descent defined in different ways under the Indian Act (e.g., Status vs. Non-Status Indians). Although the term *Indian* has lost favour outside of its use in the Indian Act, and can be used in a derogatory sense, some First Nations people still use it to refer to themselves.

Indian day schools are not as well known as residential schools, but these were also racially segregated schools for Aboriginal children that operated across Canada. As with residential schools, the focus was on assimilation. Speaking an Aboriginal language was forbidden, and students learned to be ashamed of their culture. The same institutions that were responsible for running the day schools ran the residential schools, and the same sorts of abuses happened at both.

Indian hospitals were racially segregated hospitals across Canada that for decades (until the 1970s) treated only Aboriginal people, mostly for tuberculosis. They were opened as a way of protecting white Canadians from infection. Many patients stayed at these hospitals for years, suffering not only from their disease but also from separation from their families, isolation, strict confinement and even abuse. The hospitals operated at half the cost of white hospitals and often had inadequate, poorly trained staff and inferior medical treatment.

The *Indian student room* is a room set aside in many high schools as a specific gathering place for Aboriginal students. A staff member of Aboriginal ancestry is often assigned to the room to support students.

The term *Indigenous*, generally used in an international context, refers to peoples who are the original inhabitants of a particular territory. This term is very similar to *Aboriginal* and has a positive connotation.

Internalized racism occurs when people targeted by racism, overt or covert, begin to believe the racist comments, feel ashamed of their ancestry and often then become racist towards their own people.

Lakota are members of the Sioux Nation. The word *Lakota* means "considered friends."

The *Medicine Wheel* represents the sacred circle of life. While the aspects and teachings of the wheel may vary among Nations, there are common principles.

Métis are people of mixed First Nations and European ancestry, as distinct from First Nations, Inuit or non-Aboriginals. The Métis have a unique culture and language that draws on their diverse ancestral origins.

Michif is the traditional language of the Métis.

Native is a term that was commonly used in the 1980s and '90s to describe the original inhabitants of Canada. Some Indigenous people in Canada still prefer this term.

The *Ojibway* Nation is one of the largest in Canada and the United States and is part of the Anishinaabe-speaking peoples.

Party lines were shared telephone lines common in rural areas for many years.

Pipe Carriers carry a pipe on behalf of the people. They use the pipe to pray for the people, to call in the spirits for a gathering or ceremony, and for healing or teaching.

A *Pow Wow* is a gathering at which Aboriginal people celebrate their rich heritage, socialize with old friends and make new friends. It is set up in a circle, with the drummers singing different styles of songs for the dancers and for Grand Entry.

Rat root (also called sweet flag) is a traditional medicine often used to help relieve gas and stomach cramps and clear nasal and respiratory passages. It also helps to clear the mind.

Reserves are those lands set apart for the use and benefit of a First Nation band, and for which the legal title rests with the Crown in right of Canada.

Residential schools were boarding schools for Aboriginal children that operated in Canada from the late nineteenth century through almost the entire twentieth century. They were intended to assimilate the children of Aboriginal peoples into European-Canadian society. The effect of the schools, which forcibly separated children from their families and often subjected them to abuse, has been described as cultural genocide, or "killing the Indian in the child."

Ribbon shirts are often worn for ceremonial and other formal occasions. They have usually been received as gifts, reflecting the values of generosity, honour and bravery.

Sage is a traditional medicine used for releasing what is troubling the mind and for removing negative energy. It is also used for cleansing homes and sacred items. Some believe sage is more medicinal than sweetgrass, so it is frequently used in ceremonies. You can boil sage and drink it as a tea.

Saskabush is a slang term for the province of Saskatchewan.

The **Secwepemc** Nation (anglicized as "Shuswap") is a Salish people with seventeen bands over a large territory in the south-central interior of B.C.

Sixties Scoop refers to the enforced adoption of First Nations and Métis children in Canada between the early 1960s and the mid-1980s. The period is so named because, in many instances, children were "scooped," literally taken, from their homes and communities without the prior knowledge or consent of their families or bands. The majority of those adopted were placed in non-Aboriginal homes.

A *smudge bowl*, usually a shell, holds traditional medicines (smudge) for burning.

Smudging is a way of cleansing your spirit to clear negative energy and strengthen positive energy and clear thinking. The forms of smudging can vary, but it usually involves burning traditional medicines (sage, sweetgrass, cedar and/or tobacco) and brushing the smoke over your body.

The *spirit world*, also known as the other side, is where the spirits of the Ancestors reside.

Squaw is a derogatory term for an Aboriginal woman.

Star blankets tell a story through their diamond-shaped sections. The traditional colours of yellow, red, black and white seen in many Star blankets represent the four directions, the four races and the four stages of life. Star blankets are often given to people during life-changing events as gifts of respect, honour and protection.

A *Sunrise Ceremony* is held at dawn and usually led by an Elder. Some ceremonies include a sacred fire and/or a pipe. The rising sun is honoured, and the Creator is thanked for the opportunity of the new day.

The *sweat lodge* ("sweat" for short) represents the womb of Mother Earth. The sweat lodge and the ceremonies that take place in it are sacred, intended for spiritual healing and purification of the body, mind, soul and spirit. The ceremonies vary from Nation to Nation but often include prayers, drumming and offerings to the spirit world.

Sweetgrass is one of the four traditional medicines (along with sage, cedar and tobacco) used for smudging and purification of the spirit. Sweetgrass is believed to attract positivity and is known by some Nations as the sacred hair of Mother Earth. It has a sweet aroma and is braided into three strands representing love, kindness and honesty.

Tobacco is used as an offering for prayer and in every ceremony. A tobacco offering can be made through fire, so that the smoke can lift your prayers; it can be set on the ground in a clean place; or it can be offered to an Elder or someone from whom you are requesting knowledge, advice or help.

Traditional medicines are plant- or animal-based medicines used within a culture for countless generations to treat, diagnose and prevent illnesses and/or maintain well-being.

Traditional teachings are the information that is passed down from generation to generation, usually by Elders and healers. The teachings are often shared through storytelling.

Tuberculosis (TB) is an infectious disease that typically attacks the lungs but can also affect other parts of the body. It was rampant in residential schools, and many students spent years in Indian hospitals. Some recovered, but, unfortunately, many succumbed to the disease.

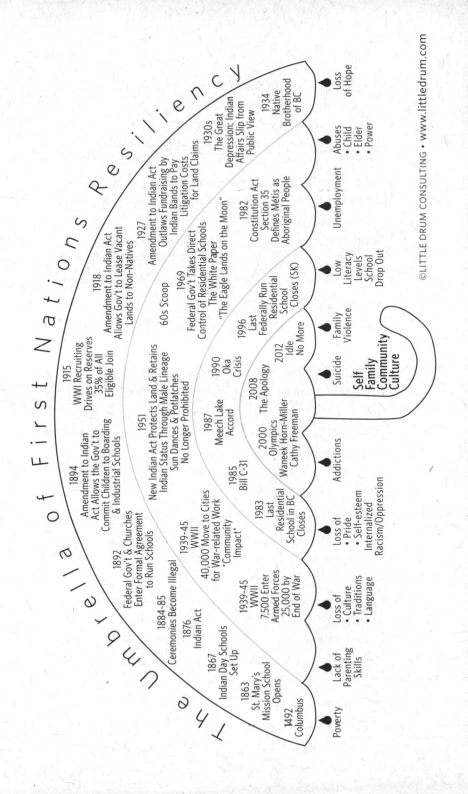

The Umbrella of First Nations Resiliency

©LITTLE DRUM CONSULTING • www.littledrum.com

1492
Columbus

1863
St. Mary's
Mission School
Opens

1867
Indian Day Schools
Set Up

1876
Indian Act

1884-85
Ceremonies Become Illegal

1892
Federal Gov't & Churches
Enter Formal Agreement
to Run Schools

1894
Amendment to Indian
Act Allows the Gov't to
Commit Children to Boarding
& Industrial Schools

1915
WWI Recruiting
Drives on Reserves
35% of All
Eligible Join

1918
Amendment to Indian Act
Allows Gov't to Lease Vacant
Lands to Non-Natives

1927
Amendment to Indian Act
Outlaws Fundraising by
Indian Bands to Pay
Litigation Costs
for Land Claims

1930s
The Great
Depression; Indian
Affairs Slip from
Public View

1934
Native
Brotherhood
of BC

1939-45
WWII
7,500 Enter
Armed Forces
25,000 by
End of War

1939-45
WWII
40,000 Move to Cities
for War-related Work
*Community
Impact*

1951
New Indian Act Protects Land & Retains
Indian Status Through Male Lineage
Sun Dances & Potlatches
No Longer Prohibited

1969
Federal Gov't Takes Direct
Control of Residential Schools
The White Paper
'"The Eagle Lands on the Moon"

60s Scoop

1982
Constitution Act
Section 35
Defines Métis as
Aboriginal People

1983
Last
Residential
School in BC
Closes

1985
Bill C-31

1987
Meech Lake
Accord

1990
Oka
Crisis

1996
Last
Federally Run
Residential
School
Closes (SK)

2000
Olympics
Waneek Horn-Miller
Cathy Freeman

2008
The Apology

2012
Idle
No More

Self
Family
Community
Culture

Poverty

Lack of
Parenting
Skills

Loss of
• Culture
• Traditions
• Language

Loss of
• Pride
• Self-esteem
Internalized
Racism/Oppression

Addictions

Suicide

Family
Violence

Low
Literacy
Levels
School
Drop Out

Unemployment

Abuses
• Child
• Elder
• Power

Loss
of Hope

QUESTIONS FOR DISCUSSION

1. *Tilly: A Story of Hope and Resilience* is published as a work of creative non-fiction. Why do you think the author chose to fictionalize her own story? How far from the truth can a memoir stray before it becomes a work of fiction?

2. Why does the author choose to begin Tilly's story with the scene she does? How does this opening relate to the final scene in the book in which Dan first meets his great-grandchild?

3. What is the significance of the dragonfly in the story?

4. How would you describe Tilly's relationships with her family members?

5. Which characters do you identify with the most? The least? How come?

6. Throughout, the author integrates information about the history of Aboriginal peoples in Canada. What did you learn about this history over the course of the story?

7. In what ways is Tilly similar to Grandma Tilly?

8. What is the significance of Tilly's fishing trip with Grandma Tilly? How do you think her influence shapes Tilly?

9. When Auntie Pauline tells Tilly that she is moving away, she recalls words from Grandma Tilly: "Wherever you go, there you are." In what ways is this true?

10. What are some of your reactions to Chapter 31, Tears Are Medicine?

11. Dreams play an important role in the book. Discuss the idea that dreams experienced during different parts of the night relate to the dreamer's past, present and future.

12. Though Aboriginal peoples in Canada have faced many challenges, the author says, "[The fact] we are thriving in the multitude of ways we are is pure inspiration." What aspects of Aboriginal communities and culture contribute to their resilience?

13. Tilly is of Cree, Lakota and Scottish ancestry, but the message of pursuing one's "dreams, ambitions and heart's desires" is universal. How does this message resonate in your own life?

ABOUT THE AUTHOR

Monique Gray Smith is a mixed-heritage woman of Cree, Lakota and Scottish ancestry and a proud mom of young twins. Under the umbrella of her own business, Little Drum Consulting, Monique is an accomplished consultant, writer and international speaker. She is well known for her warmth, spirit of generosity and focus on resilience. Monique has been sober and involved in her healing journey for over twenty years. She and her family are blessed to live on Coast Salish territory in Victoria, B.C.